REPORTAGE PRESS

ABOUT THE AUTHOR

Journalist and writer Tim Judah is known for his reporting of the Balkans, but he has long reported from Africa too. After graduating from the London School of Economics and the Fletcher School of Law and Diplomacy, he joined the *BBC African Service*. Since then he has reported from many of the world's trouble spots including Afghanistan, Bosnia, Kosovo, Darfur, Uganda and Iraq. Although Judah has followed the conflicts in the former Yugoslavia for almost two decades, mostly for *The Economist*, he has maintained a keen interest in African politics. He has broadcast widely and written for the *New York Review of Books*, the *Observer*, the *Sunday Telegraph Magazine*, *Granta* and the *Times*. Judah is also the author of the prize-winning *The Serbs: History, Myth and the Destruction of Yugoslavia*, *Kosovo: War and Revenge* and *Kosovo: What Everyone Needs to Know*. He lives in London with his wife and five children.

BIKILA

ETHIOPIA'S BAREFOOT OLYMPIAN

BY TIM JUDAH

REPORTAGE PRESS

· REPORTAGE PRESS

Reportage Press
26 Richmond Way, London W12 8LY, United Kingdom.
Tel: + 44 7971 461 935
Fax: + 44 20 8749 2867
e-mail: info@reportagepress.com
www.reportagepress.com

Published by Reportage Press, 2008

Bikila: Ethiopia's Barefoot Olympian was produced under the editorial direction
of Laura Keeling

For permission to reprint extracts from copyright material the author gratefully
acknowledges the following: C.Hurst & Co, (Publishers) Ltd, for extracts from Hans
Wilhelm Lockot's The Mission: The Life, Reign and Character of Emperor Haile
Selassie I, (London 1992). Tsige Abebe, for extracts from: Triumph & Tragedy (Addis
Ababa, 1996). Tadele Yidnekatchew Tessema for extracts from: Yidnekatchew Tessema
(1921-1987): In the World and in the World of Sports, (Addis Ababa, 1997). Prof
Bahru Zewde for an extract from A History of Modern Ethiopia: 1855-1974, (London
& Addis Ababa, 1995). Tadeletch Zegeye Wahlborg for extracts from Ragnhild Wa-
hlborg's Our Way to a Better Life. (Unpublished, undated manuscript, approx. 1975,
which is a translation of Mina tio an i en lepraby / My Ten Years in the Leprosy Village
which was published in Sweden.) Neil Allen for extracts from his books; Olympic
Diary: Rome 1960 (London 1960) and Olympic Diary: Tokyo 1964 (London 1965).

Every effort has been made to trace and contact copyright holders.
The publishers will be pleased to correct any omissions or mistakes in future editions.

British Library Cataloguing in Publication Data.

A catalogue record for this book is available from the British Library.

Hardback Edition ISBN-13: 978-0-9558302-4-2
Paperback Edition ISBN-13: 978-0-9558302-1-1

Cover design by Joshua Haymann
Layout by Marine Galtier

Printed and bound in Great Britain by CPI Antony Rowe, Chippenham, Wiltshire
www.antonyrowe.co.uk

For Renaud Girard, with thanks.

For Reginald Carroll, with thanks.

Barefoot Bikila First at Rome in Fastest Olympic Marathon

By ALLISON DANZIG
Special to The New York Times.

ROME, Sept. 10—A skinny, barefooted palace guard in the Ethiopian Army of King Haile Selassie ran the fastest marathon in history tonight.

A rank outsider who never had run the distance of 26 miles 385 yards outside his own country, 28-year-old Abebe Bikila won the classic race of the Olympic Games over a course rich in history.

It started at Campidoglio Square, designed by Michelangelo, skirted the Circus Maximus and the Baths of Caracalla, went along the 2,000-year-old Appian Way and ended at the Arch of Constantine.

As the lean, little Ethiopian approached the brilliantly illuminated arch, close by the ruins of the Forum and Colosseum, thousands cheered.

Running strongly, the green-shirted Bikila finished 25.4 seconds ahead of favored Abdeslam Rhadi of Morocco. He had held the lead with Rhadi from slightly before the halfway mark until he went out in front alone with 1,000 meters to go.

"We Abyssinians are a poor people with no mechanical transport ... So we run everywhere on foot. Forty kilometres are nothing to me."

Abebe Bikila on winning the Rome marathon, 1960.

CONTENTS

CONTENT

Notes and Acknowledgements

Most of the research for this book was done in 1997 and 1998 but, until now, it was not written up as such. I went to Ethiopia, to Rome, to Sweden, to France and to the International Olympic Committee in Lausanne in Switzerland to interview people about Bikila and Niskanen. They gave generously of their time, especially the Niskanen family. Some are no longer living. In Stockholm, Lorenzo Nesi, a journalist and marathon runner, did invaluable archive research. In 2008, Marianne Sautermeister, Niskanen's niece, put me back in touch with the rest of the family.

Bikila's daughter, Tsige Bikila, who was very young when he died, has written a fascinating book about her father called *Triumph and Tragedy*. I have quoted from it several times and I am extremely grateful for her permission to do so.

This book would not have happened if it had not been for the role played by Renaud Girard, *grand reporter*, at the *Figaro*.

Especially helpful was Tadele Yidnekatchew Tessema, whose father, Yidnekatchew Tessema, played a key role in developing Ethiopian and African sports. Much valuable archival material on his father and the period can be found on his website: www.tessemas.net.

After he died Onni Niskanen's photo album was left to *Radda Barnen* – Swedish Save the Children in Ethiopia. Two thirds of the illustrations in the book come from there and for that I am extremely grateful. Some of them have never been seen before. They are the ones marked "Niskanen Collection". Unfortunately, Niskanen wrote nothing by his pictures, which explains why we don't know when or where many of them were taken.

A further note on sources and also a list of many of the people interviewed for this book can be found at the end.

A note on names and dates: Ethiopians do not have surnames. They have a given name and the name of their father. Bikila is thus "Abebe, son of Bikila."

Sometimes dates given by different people in different accounts of events in Bikila's life vary. One reason for this may be confusion deriving from the fact that the Ethiopians use their own Coptic, Christian Orthodox calendar, which in turn is based on that used by the ancient Egyptians. Depending on the time of year, this means that Ethiopia is seven or eight years "behind" that of the rest of the world. For example, Ethiopians only celebrated the first day of the new millennium on 12 September 2007. They also have 13 months instead of twelve. To make matters even more complicated the Ethiopian clock is also different. Our 7.00 am is their 1.00 am; our midday is their 6.00 am and so on.

As with all books published by Reportage Press, part of the proceeds will go to charity. In this case it is the Ethiopia Programme of *Radda Barnen*, which is Sweden's Save the Children. I chose it because from 1972 to 1981 it was headed by Onni Niskanen, who then continued to advise it until his death. Save the Children Sweden works in close cooperation with Save the Children Ethiopia, which explains the background to its mission thus:

> Children in Ethiopia are growing up in one of the world's poorest countries. Most Ethiopians still earn a living from the land, and even in a good year millions of families cannot produce enough food. In years of bad harvests, hunger quickly escalates into food crises with widespread malnutrition. This is made worse by lack of access to services such as healthcare, education, water and sanitation. In addition, the HIV/AIDS pandemic is sweeping Ethiopia; it has the world's third highest number of people infected with HIV. Harmful traditional practices like early marriage and female genital mutilation are widespread.

Tim Judah
London 2008

Preface

On 10 September 1960, Abebe Bikila, an Ethiopian, won the Rome Olympic marathon running barefoot. He thus became a sporting hero, an African hero and, for many, the first black African they had ever heard of.

It was a famous victory. Bikila was the first black African ever to win a gold medal at the Olympics. Four years later in Tokyo, he was to repeat his success. This, the athlete's tale, would make for a good story alone. But there is a far better one here. The story of Abebe Bikila turns the tale of an African champion runner into that of a man of his times. Almost half a century later it remains as powerful and fascinating as ever.

Today, Haile Gebreselassie and many others from Ethiopia, Kenya and Eritrea are well known as some of the fastest runners on earth. But, this was not the case until Bikila won in Rome. He was the trailblazer. It was only then that the relationship between living at high altitude, the lungs, running and endurance began to be understood.

From the very beginning, the Bikila story was about far more than science and training. It was one laden with symbolism. Exactly 25 years before Bikila took his first Olympic gold, Fascist Italy had set out to recreate a new

Roman Empire by conquering Ethiopia. But the symbolism of the victory of Emperor Haile Selassie's barefoot guardsman in Rome did not stop there. From that day on Bikila was to become a shooting star, burning fast and bright before fading away into the firmament.

Bikila was a man who, to many, appeared mild-mannered. But this was deceptive; he had a steely determination. He wanted, of course, to run to win. But, unwittingly, he became a legend in his own lifetime and a symbol for the new Africa in its years of decolonisation and hope. By the time of his tragic death in 1973, the continent's dreams were shattered and Ethiopia was on the brink of famine, revolution, war and destruction.

Today Bikila is well remembered as a sporting hero, although much of his true story has never been told. Much of that tale though is also that of another man - a Swede called Onni Niskanen, who was Bikila's trainer. Now he is mostly forgotten, or rather, he was never in the limelight. He was a soldier, an adventurer and a man who changed the history of sport. Just like Bikila, his own life and times are what make the tale of this man so extraordinary, and the story of the two of them together so unlikely. In 1940, when Bikila was seven-years-old, probably herding goats and sheep, Niskanen left a comfy middle class life in Stockholm to volunteer to fight for Finland in its war against the Soviet Union.

So this is also the story of how the paths of these two men came to cross. Their backgrounds and experience could hardly have been more different. And yet together, they planned to take on the sporting world. Bikila was the athlete and the champion but Niskanen was the architect of his success. Twenty years after Niskanen had taken that train to the Finnish front, Bikila took the Olympics by storm and shattered all the records. Theirs was the most unlikely of friendships and yet their success dazzled the world.

Niskanen was a man of burning ambition. From his youth in Sweden he had dreamed of sporting gold. It was not to be. In Ethiopia though, he struck a different kind of gold. Here he discovered the fastest men on earth – in the service of an emperor who traced his line to the legend of King Solomon and the Queen of Sheba. If Niskanen could not be the fastest man on earth, then he would make the men who would. He was an exuberant showman full of life and love. He was also a man of the noblest intentions who devoted his life to helping Ethiopia and its people. "He's more of an Ethiopian than you are!" scoffed the Emperor Haile Selassie, speaking about him to Ethiopian coaches.

From Marathon to Shepherd's Bush

The marathon; quite literally the stuff of legend. In 490 BC, a small Athenian army defeated the Persians at the town of Marathon. Then, says the legend, Pheidippides the messenger ran all the way to Athens, exclaimed "We were victorious!" and promptly dropped down dead. But is it true? Who knows? Some historians give different names to the messenger, while others name Pheidippides as the herald who ran not from Marathon to Athens but rather from Athens to Sparta.

In 1876, the poet Robert Browning wrote a poem about Pheidippides and the run from Marathon. It inspired a generation. The founder of the modern Olympics, Baron Pierre de Coubertin, was much taken with the idea, proposed to him by Michel Bréal, a French philologist, that in the first games, to be held in Athens in 1896, men should run from Marathon, about 40 kilometres away, by the longer of two routes.

The first victor was the water-carrier Spiridon Louis. It took him 2 hours 58 minutes and 50 seconds.

From then on the idea took off. For the first few years, however, the actual length of the race varied. In 1908, it was set at 42.195 kilometres or 26.22 miles, which was the exact distance from the east lawn of Windsor

Castle to the White City Stadium in Shepherd's Bush, west London. An extra 385 yards were added inside the stadium, so that the London Olympic run could end in front of the royal box.

In the next two Olympic games the length of the run varied again. But in 1924 for the Paris games, which were attended by Ras Tafari, the future Emperor Haile Selassie of Ethiopia, it was finally settled. Ever since then the length for the marathon has been set as it was in London in 1908.

1. Beginnings

There are no clues in Bikila's early life to suggest that he was marked for greatness. He was born on 7 August 1932 in Jatto, a tiny village, if that, in the Debre Berhan district of Shoa, an area some two to three hours drive north of Addis Ababa, the Ethiopian capital.

On the other side of the world, on exactly the same day, the Argentine Juan Carlos Zabala thrilled spectators by winning the gold medal in the marathon in the Los Angeles Olympics.

Even today Jatto is hard to get to. It is far from any paved road and lies in a remote countryside of rolling hills. The soil is rich but rocky and cars can easily get bogged down on the mud tracks. Apart from *teff*, a unique form of Ethiopian wheat, it is cattle and wool country. There are no fences to break the landscape, which is dotted with trees and haystacks and peasants herding their cows and sheep. More often than not this job is the preserve of barefoot children. Over the horizon, groups can be seen riding their richly decorated horses. If the sun is high they shade themselves with colourful umbrellas. In the countryside nobody owns a car and there are few roads anyway.

The only form of house in the area is the classic *tukul*

or round, straw-roofed mud hut. Bikila, who sprang from peasant stock, lived and grew up in one of these. *Tukul* clusters spot the countryside and crown the low-lying hills. As night falls smoke pours through their straw roofs from charcoal braziers as the women prepare *Wat* – a spicy vegetable or meat stew – and *Injera* – flat bread on which it is served and eaten.

Bikila's name means: "Shoot, burst into blossom". According to the book written by Tsige Abebe, Bikila's daughter, her father was the son of Bikila Demissie and Wudinesh Beneberu. She writes that when Bikila was three-years-old Wudinesh divorced her husband "because he was too young for her" and married her third husband, Temtime Kefelew. Not that much is known about his earliest years, but then they appear to have been unremarkable. He was, after all, just the small son of peasant farmers, growing up in the Ethiopian highlands, as had countless generations before him.

In 1964, in the run up to the Tokyo Olympics, *World Sports* magazine sent Colin Gibson to Ethiopia to interview and observe Bikila and his friend and rival Mamo Wolde in training. He wrote that, "as a barefoot young shepherd-boy minding his family's herds, Bikila was used to walking and running several miles every day in search of grazing on the lava-strewn crags surrounding his home. At 13 he went to school and played *ganna*, Ethiopia's long-distance version of hockey, with the goalposts in the opposing teams' villages – maybe a couple of miles apart."

By tradition *ganna* is played at Christmas, with which it shares its name. It is a rough and tumble game played between village teams. Ethiopian Orthodox Christians remember the birth of Christ, like most other Orthodox, on January 7th. The story goes that *ganna* was invented when Ethiopian shepherds celebrated the birth of Jesus by turning round their crooks and using them as hockey sticks.

In 1932, Ethiopia's prestige was high, both in Africa and other parts of the colonial world. Along with Liberia, it was the only independent black African state. This is no irrelevant detail. Three years after Bikila's birth, Mussolini's troops began their conquest of the country, using poison gas.

Immediately Ethiopia became an international cause célèbre. Indelibly printed on the minds of those who lived through these turbulent times is the image of the stern-faced Emperor, Haile Selassie, standing at the bar of the League of Nations in Geneva pleading his country's case. The failure of the international community to act robustly over Ethiopia is often cited as one of the many steps on the road to world war. "God and history will remember your judgement," he said. Then he reminded the members of the League and the great powers that they had promised a guarantee of collective security to small countries, "on whom weighs the threat that they may one day suffer the fate of Ethiopia."

> I ask, what measures do you intend to take? Representatives of the world, I have come to Geneva to discharge in your midst the most painful of the duties of the head of a State. What reply shall I have to take back to my people?

The answer was a resounding silence. In the meantime, Mussolini could claim that a great stain on Italy's national conscience – the crushing defeat of Italian troops at the hands of the Ethiopians at Adowa in 1896 – had been expunged. He also told the world that his "Fascist Empire" was an "Empire of Peace". Of course it was nothing of the sort and the next few years were to see a drama of unprecedented proportions unroll across the mountains and plains of Ethiopia.

Tsige Abebe writes that, because of the invasion, Bikila's village was occupied by Italian troops and that his family had to flee to another even more remote hamlet called Gorro. Although the family might have had to seek shelter in Gorro the idea that Jatto was occupied would seem unlikely. Even if the Italians could have been bothered to get to this mud hut cluster, it is inconceivable that they would have had any reason to stay. Nevertheless, it is true that the Italians never properly occupied the whole of Ethiopia, least of all the countryside, so fighting in the area might well have caused a temporary dislocation of the local peasantry.

Following Bikila's triumph in Rome in 1960, one report noted that his father had been an anti-Italian guerrilla. There is no evidence to support this. In fact, Bikila seems to have lost contact with his father. After the liberation in 1941, the family returned to Jatto, or possibly nearby Jirru, where they certainly lived later.

Bikila's basic education would have been at a church school where he would have learned to read and write - if little else. Like all other children, then and now, Bikila would then have spent the rest of his day, as Colin Gibson noted, herding the family cattle.

Although Bikila's mother's name is Amharic, Jatto is an Oromo speaking area. At the time, Amharas constituted the bulk of the ruling class of Ethiopia. Although some 40% of the population were Oromo they were regarded as backward peasants. Amharic was then the only official language of Ethiopia and is mutually unintelligible from Oromo. Bikila grew up speaking Oromo but clearly learned Amharic as well. The significance of this is that Bikila was later looked down upon by the snobbish elite of Addis Ababa, some of whom found him difficult to understand because of his thick Oromo peasant accent.

From 1936 to 1941, Haile Selassie went into exile in Britain, residing in the spa town of Bath. After the British had driven the Italians out of his country and their neighbouring colony of Eritrea, Selassie returned to the throne in triumph. After the war, Eritrea, which had been an Italian colony since 1890, was federated to Ethiopia. But it was Selassie's high-handed treatment of the Eritreans and the abolition of their autonomy which were to sow the seeds of Ethiopia's own destruction and the 30 year struggle for Eritrean independence.

At about the age of 19, in 1951, Bikila moved to Addis Ababa to follow his mother who now lived there. According to Tsige Abebe, he was unemployed for a year but then joined the Imperial Bodyguard, the elite corps detailed to secure the Emperor's protection. Bikila chose the Bodyguard for several reasons. Firstly, it was the most prestigious part of the armed forces. It was modelled, in part, on the Guards regiments of the British Army. For many young men of humble backgrounds it was a route out of the provinces and into a secure career. This was actively encouraged by the Emperor who, according to the memoir of Hans Wilhelm Lockot, who worked for many years in Addis Ababa, asked "for searches to be made of boys in the lower grades for the best achievers in school-work and those who showed exceptional natural talent in other ways." These boys were then presented to the Emperor, "and if his impressions were favourable they would be given further help through secondary school." Many joined the Guards via this route.

Wami Biratu was another Oromo peasant turned Guardsman marathon runner. When Bikila joined the Guards, Biratu was already a member. In 1997, he was a sprightly 80-year-old and lived in a modest house in Addis Ababa surrounded by his large family and pictures of his glory days. Proudly displayed was one photograph of him receiving an award from a smiling Emperor and another of Bikila shaking hands with the commander of the Imperial Bodyguard.

Wami explained that a big reason for wanting to become a member of the Guards was that in peacetime, unlike other parts of the army, they stayed in Addis Ababa. In other words, they were not despatched to remote and desolate provinces, nor were they detailed to guard the country's frontiers. "You had to be tall, strong, aggressive, clean and alert," recalled Biratu, "and you got to guard the palace." Another attraction was the possibilities it offered for such sports as horse riding.

There was, however, another important reason why Bikila joined the Guards. His half-brother, Kinfe Bikila, was already a member. Although the Guards were actively recruiting at this stage, because contingents were being sent to fight in Korea, it is certain that Kinfe used his influence to secure his brother's enlistment. Bikila joined the 5th Infantry Regiment. Photographs show him wearing the Guards' characteristic pith helmet, Star of David arm flashes and Lion of Judah symbols. These underscored the claim that Haile Selassie was descended from the biblical union of King Solomon and the Queen of Sheba – the central guiding myth of Ethiopian Christian Orthodox civilisation.

The Ethiopia of the 1950s was a relatively quiet country. This meant that the Imperial Guard were neither consumed by plots nor by having to put down rebellions. For a simple and athletic man like Bikila these were halcyon days. *World Sports* reported that, "In his first four years of army life the young private played football, volleyball and basketball, and it was not until late 1956 that he took up running. He met with instant success, coming second to the national long-distance champion, Wami Biratu, in the army marathon." What was it that made the football mad Bikila turn to running? The answer is that he had been spotted by Onni Niskanen, the Guard's Swedish sport's trainer. Michael Lentakis, a Greek who was born and lived in Ethiopia at the time, writes, in his fascinating and at times boisterous memoir, that Niskanen had, "seen this solider running from Sululta to Addis and back everyday and hit upon the idea of letting him try the marathon." Sululta is a hilly area more than 20 kilometres north of Addis Ababa and so it seems Bikila was living here at the time.

Tsige Abebe paints an interesting vignette of this period. While she says that her father's main sporting interest at this time was football, she adds that he noticed, while training, that another group of sportsmen were dressed in better quality outfits and tracksuits.

They were the sportsmen who, like Mamo Wolde and Hailu Abebe, had participated in the 1956 Olympic games in Melbourne. Tsige writes that they were regarded with "exceptional admiration" not just because they had represented Ethiopia at the Olympics but because they had had a chance to go abroad. So Bikila began to tell his friends that he too would go abroad to compete. "He said this only to become a laughing stock among his colleagues, who remarked cynically that not any odd soul would make it ...That ridicule and the humiliating comments of his friends provoked in his thoughts a certain strange feeling and sensation. He secretly vowed to himself to work hard and to prepare himself for the competition."

When he was off duty Bikila played a *krar*, the distinctive five or six-stringed musical instrument typical of Ethiopia and Eritrea. He also now played less football and, probably encouraged by Niskanen, began to run more. Wudinesh, his mother, disapproved. She thought that running was a very unpromising avenue to success. She tried giving him less food in a bid to wean him off running but eventually settled on the notion that her son had to be married. She reasoned that once he settled down and had the responsibility of looking after a family he would stop wasting time on the track. She lined him up with 15-year-old Yewebdar Wolde Giorgis. This was an arrangement for an arranged marriage that worked. The two were married on 16 March 1960. The second part of Wudinesh's plan, to distract Bikila from running by marriage was, of course, a failure.

2. Onni Goes to Addis

When Bikila stormed to victory at the Rome Olympics of 1960 the world's sporting establishment, including the journalists who covered the event, were shocked. Who was this Ethiopian and where on earth had he sprung from? There was one man who had the answer: Onni Niskanen. The man's background was so utterly different from that of Bikila that he might have come from Mars let alone the cold lands of the north. The curious thing is, of course, that if fate had not brought these two together, neither would be remembered today. The two became inextricably linked in life and now in memory. Without Niskanen there would have been no champion Bikila and, in its own way, Niskanen's story is just as fascinating as that of the runner.

Kept in the office of Save the Children in Addis Ababa is Onni Niskanen's photo album. It is a typical old-fashioned one with pictures coming loose here and there. Here he is in the 1930s, a young athlete. Here he is in military uniform in a wood. An officer appears to be pinning a medal on him. Is he deep inside the Soviet Union? We do not know as nothing is written beneath the pictures. Here he is in his 70s wearing a party hat and here he is again, massaging the legs of Bikila, his favourite protégé. Here is Niskanen the balloonist, the rally driver, a young man with pretty girls, a soldier, a bridegroom, the director of Addis Ababa's leprosy hospital and here is his pass for the Stockholm underground.[1]

Few people live as full a life as Niskanen. This was a man who knew how to enjoy himself and push himself to the limit. But Niskanen had one distinctive feature. He was also a man who liked secrets and order. Ulf Niskanen, his nephew, says that the paradox of his uncle was that he, "liked control but he also had a side to him which just wanted to let things go."

As Niskanen emerges from the shadows of the past, it is clear that he was a person who lived several lives at once. He did not live a proverbial double life – he was far more complex a character than that. He was a man who, at his prime, lived at least three utterly separate lives at the same time. While this makes him a fascinating study it also makes him hard to research, because those that thought they knew him, in fact knew only part of him. They knew nothing of his other lives or the people that lived there.

Onni Herman Niskanen was born on 31 August 1910 in Helsinki. His father, Waino, owned a printing house and was of Finno-Swedish origin. His mother, Hulda Josefina, was a Swede born in the central western Swedish region of Varmland in the small village of Blekvattnet. Onni had three brothers, only one of whom, Erik, is still alive.

In 1910, the Grand Duchy of Finland was still part of the Russian Empire. The Niskanens lived in a large flat just above the local Russian military commander. Niskanen senior had had some experience of the Russian

---

1. *Many of the illustrations in this book come from this album.*

military. In his youth, he had attended cadet school in St Petersburg.

In 1913, Waino decided on a prudent course of action to avoid being drafted if war broke out. He moved his family to Solna, a northern suburb of Stockholm, which had, incidentally, staged the Olympics the year before. The move itself was not without some little drama which, being three-years-old, Onni might just have remembered. As the ferry sailed from Helsinki harbour, the horrified family realised that they had left thirteen-day-old Erik behind. The ferry was turned around and Erik rescued from the kitchen of their old home where he had been forgotten.

In Solna, the boys grew up taking an early interest in sports and scouting. In the 1930s, according to Erik: "the Niskanen brothers were quite well known" in sporting circles. The three younger brothers competed in several sports; walking, track running, cross-country, orienteering and skiing. The youngest brother, Arne, competed in the Swedish walking championships, while Onni excelled in cross-country.

According to Erik, who in his old age lives in a cosy house in the small, central Swedish town of Mora surrounded by souvenirs from Ethiopia, the brothers got on well together and each had their own clear interests. The oldest brother, Waino, had his motorbike, Onni was interested in sport, Erik was a scout and Arne was interested in business.

Sven Strandberg was one of Onni's oldest friends from his youth. He recalls that they began their sporting career together in a club called *Huvudsta IS* in 1928. *Huvudsta* proved not to be to their liking though. There

was a specific reason for this. It had many up and coming boxers and since there was money in boxing the
club invested in them, leaving the runners without coaches. Since Standberg and Niskanen both had girlfriends
in another club, a small one called *Duvbo IK*, they decided to move there.

Although he loved sports and was good at them, Niskanen was not the stuff of champions. From the records
of *Duvbo* we have the following: Niskanen was first
mentioned in the records in 1930. His results were 16
minutes 53.4 seconds in the 5,000 metres and 4 minutes 32 seconds in the 1,500 metres. Later he produced
good results in cross-country running and orienteering.
In 1933, he broke the club record in the 10,000 metres
with a time of 34 minutes 10 seconds. In 1936, he won
the "club championships" with 55.2 seconds in the 400
metres and 2 minutes 5.7 seconds in the 800 metres.
However, with every passing year Niskanen's times im-
proved and, in 1937, he became president of *Duvbo*.

Photos from Niskanen's album show him running and
also include a picture of an elderly man preparing a running track. From 1935, we have an identification card
showing Niskanen in military uniform. It says "With
Memories of S.S. Roserberg," which was a military cadet school which Niskanen attended.

In 1936, Niskanen embarked on a particular adventure. The Olympics, which had been awarded to Germany
in 1931 and which were to begin on August 1st, had by
now become the Nazi games. So, the new Popular Front
government of Spain decided to organise a rival *Olim-
piada Popular* or People's Olympics in Barcelona along
with the government of autonomous Catalonia.

The Swedes who were to go were organised by the small Swedish Workers Sport Assocation. There were twelve of them including a leader, a chess player and Niskanen as a middle-distance runner. The decision to send a team was controversial in left wing circles, but nevertheless hundreds gathered to see them off at Stockholm station on July 18th. But disaster was about to strike as the day before the Spanish nationalist rebellion began and plunged the country into civil war. The Swedes got to Paris but no further.

In *Duvbo's* 1938 yearbook comes the following mention: "Onni has been running with his thumbs pointing upwards ever since he came back from England this summer. First we believed it was something he had learned from the World Champion Lovelock, but it turned out to be the 'Lambeth Walk.'" Far from being a style of running this was a kind of walking dance craze which swept Europe and America, inspired by a song of the same name from the 1937 hit musical, *Me and My Girl*. Jack Lovelock was a New Zealander who took his country's first gold medal in the Olympics in Berlin in 1936, in which he broke the world record for the 1,500 metres. Interestingly, the next year, Lovelock published a pamphlet called: *Athletics for Health: Running Theory and Practice*. Given Niskanen's future career it seems more than likely he would have bought and read this.

At some point in the late thirties, no one can seem to remember when, Niskanen married a girl called Britta Bjork. Erik says that she was a nice girl and that her parents owned a jewellery shop. The marriage lasted barely a year. It broke down because Britta presented Onni with an ultimatum. She said: "It's me or sport." Onni chose sport. In this way the die was cast. As we shall see, the fate of Onni's relationship with Britta was to determine almost all his future affairs with women.

In 1939, Onni was chosen to be *Duvbo's* "Jolly Good Fellow of the Year" or *Kalasgrabb*. This was a slightly dubious honour since Niskanen was club president, but still the citation mentioned his energy, willpower and organisational skills. They were attributes which were to stand him in good stead for almost half a century.

Before the war Niskanen began work as a typographer (he had been listed to go to Barcelona in 1935 as a member of the typographer's sport's club), but he left this to pursue a military career. On 30 November 1939, two months after the beginning of the war, the Soviet Union attacked Finland, which had refused to cede territory close to Leningrad. Along with more than 8,000 others, Niskanen joined the Swedish Volunteer Corps and went to fight for the land of his birth. Two of his brothers, including Erik, also went to fight. In the words of Neil Bruce, who knew Finland well and was to head the *BBC Finnish Service*, "their record was very distinguished."

Two of the volunteers bear particular mention here. One of the founders of the Corps was Viking Tamm. One of its pilots was the 30-year-old aviator, Count Carl Gustaf von Rosen, whose aunt had married Hermann Goring, Hitler's air force chief. This connection bore no reflection on his own political views and he was later to volunteer for the RAF, though this connection disqualified him. What links them to this story is Ethiopia. Tamm had gone to fight for Haile Selassie when Mussolini invaded. Count von Rosen too had gone, but to pilot

Red Cross flights of food and supplies.

One of the items stuck in Niskanen's album is a greeting card, which shows the Finnish and Swedish flags flying together. Perhaps it was given to Onni as he left for the front. In Swedish, it says: "Good luck in your task and may your irrepressible energy and strong will contribute to the final and just victory that we are all waiting for."

Niskanen left for the front at Salla early in 1940 and a crowd gathered in Stockholm's Central Station to see him off. Just before this, however, some of Niskanen's friends laid bets. How many of his girlfriends would show up? The winning bid was twelve. Still Sven Strandberg implies that we cannot read too much into this episode: "It was not like that. We were all fond of Onni." In fact, Strandberg is wrong. We can read a lot into this incident. For the rest of his life women were falling in love with him, but he always seemed to have something more exciting on the go.

The war was known as the "Winter War" and was fought in a harsh terrain of frozen lakes, marshes and forest. Finnish resistance to the Red Army was stronger than had been anticipated. This led to a reorganisation of the Red Army and in the first ten days of February 1940, Finnish fortifications along their so-called Mannerheim line were subjected to an extraordinarily ferocious artillery bombardment. The Finns were forced to sue for peace and, on 12 March 1940, the Treaty of Moscow was signed, by which they were forced to cede a large area of the south east of the country to the Soviet Union.

On April 9th the Germans began their invasion of Denmark and Norway from where they expelled the British expeditionary force.

Soon after the Finnish armistice, Niskanen was home on leave. He took part in the team that won the prestigious Stadsloppet relay. There is a picture of him in uniform, dated 2 June 1940, taken at Stockholm's Olympic stadium. Elsewhere, the British were completing their evacuation from Dunkirk and within two weeks, Paris had fallen. Nazi Germany seemed triumphant. For the next year, Niskanen was back with the Swedish Army.

On 22 June 1941, Germany attacked the Soviet Union. German troops were already stationed on Finnish territory and within a few days, the country was drawn into the war. This time it was known as the "War of Continuation" or the "Summer War". Niskanen volunteered for a second time. He became a platoon commander on the Hango peninsula. In 1941, a letter he had written and which had passed the censor was published in the *Duvbo* yearbook. It said: "This life is a mixture of dream and reality. And the reality is far from pleasant at this time." Lorenzo Nesi, a Swedish journalist who has studied *Duvbo's* archives, notes: "Onni is situated only a couple of hundred yards from the Russian enemy. His duty is to try to find out what is wrong with the cables. On one occasion he realises that a telephone has been connected to a mine. That could have been the end of his career ... "

In 1943, or 1944, Niskanen was injured by a Soviet hand grenade. Shrapnel splinters embedded themselves in his face, arms, hands, legs and foot. Some were still there when he died fifty years later. In Niskanen's photo album there is a picture of him in uniform, holding a crutch, flanked by four pretty, smiling nurses.

There is also a picture of the uniformed Niskanen and a girl in a wedding dress. As we know he had already been married once. But, on Christmas Eve 1943, he married again. This time his bride was 20-year-old Mary Jakobsson. Since he looks hale and hearty this may imply that he was, in fact, injured soon afterwards, in early 1944. His brother Erik is unsure of the date.

Niskanen's wedding coincided with growing demands in Finland for peace. On 19 September 1944, the Finns signed an armistice with the Soviet Union. They demanded a German evacuation and agreed to abide by the terms of the 1940 treaty. The Germans at first refused to pull out but when they did, there was a series of clashes between them and the Finns. Large parts of northern Finland, Lapland, were devastated by the Germans as they retreated.

Following his injury, Niskanen returned to Sweden. He needed a long period of rehabilitation. With the war over Niskanen left the army but remained a reserve officer. He was promoted to major on 1 November 1946. For the past year or so he had pursued two activities. With his brothers, Waino and Arne, he had set up an advertising agency. He had also been studying to be a sports instructor and graduated in 1946. All of a sudden his life took a dramatic and unexpected turn. He received a call; did he want to go to Ethiopia?

Sweden had long had relations with Ethiopia. It had been an old target for Swedish missionaries but a political relationship had also begun as early as the 1920s when Swedes had been invited to set up schools and medical facilities. In 1924, the young Ras Tafari, later to become Emperor Haile Selassie, went to Stockholm on his European tour, which had also taken him to the Olympic games in Paris where the marathon had been won by Albin Stenroos, a Finn. At the opening of the games the future Emperor had stood next to the French president.

During the Italian invasion, a Swedish Red Cross Hospital was hit by Italian bombs and back home a generation of young Swedes was horrified by what they read. One, Ragnhild Wahlborg, a young laboratory technician and nurse recalled later: "Terror, horror and helplessness filled our hearts and minds." Professor Sven Rubenson, who was to become one of the most distinguished students of Ethiopian culture and who came to the country in 1947, sums up the feeling of many when he says: "Ethiopia was the Vietnam of my youth".

It is very unlikely that it was the Vietnam of Niskanen's youth. His brother Erik confirms that he was never interested in politics. For him the lure was adventure.

After the war, Haile Selassie, not wanting to be dependent on either the Americans or the Soviet Union, re-established the Swedish connection. He was also keen to shake off the British military tutelage that had been established over the country after the expulsion of the Italians in 1941. Count von Rosen was invited back to found the Ethiopian Air Force which was based in Debre Zeit (then Bishoftu), 35 miles south of Addis Ababa. Another key figure in re-establishing the Swedish connection was Viking Tamm, now a general, who arrived in Addis Ababa early in December 1945.

General Tamm's job was to organise the Swedes who were going to take responsibility for training telecommunications workers and the police force. While the British Military Mission, consisting of about 70 officers, remained in the country, Swedish officers were also detailed to organise a cadet school for the training of officers destined for the Emperor's Imperial Bodyguard. Tamm's impression was that the Emperor wanted to transfer training responsibilities for the whole of the armed forces from the British to the Swedes as soon as possible. The British did not object, reasoning that they would prefer the Swedes to extend their influence rather than the Americans or the Soviets.

A major recruitment drive for Ethiopia began in Sweden in 1946. This was accompanied by a Swedish government grant to pay the salaries of a contingent of up to 700 people. They were teachers, doctors and nurses who were to build up the educational and medical organisations as well as officers in charge of the newly established air force and military academies. They all came on short-term contracts.

As a reserve officer and trained sports instructor with plenty of friends in the military and sporting worlds, Niskanen was clearly an ideal choice. He may even have been called by General Tamm himself to come and teach physical education at the Cadet School.

Niskanen and Mary discussed the offer and, after a month, they decided to accept. His two-year contract was signed in the presence of the Ethiopian consul in Stockholm, one Dr Fride Hylander. They sold their flat and began to pack their belongings. The journey to Addis Ababa took the Niskanens via Amsterdam, Rome and Cairo. It was full of adventure. Niskanen has left us this account:

We had to pack everything: an iron oven, matches, enough sanitary towels for two years ... all in all we sent a package of eleven cubic metres by ship from Stockholm to Djibouti in French Somaliland. There were no flights to Addis Ababa at that time so von Rosen had the task of transporting every Swedish recruit to Addis. He flew a huge American aircraft known as a "Flying Fortress". The cabin was not pressurised. It took three days before we were in Addis.

Addis was a small town at that time, surrounded by forest-clad mountains where hyenas and jackals hid during the day. At night they would sneak down to the city in search of something to eat.

There was almost nothing to buy. We were completely dependent on the Franco-Ethiopian railway between Addis and Djibouti to get anything from abroad. The rail workers went on strike at the time of our arrival. It continued for six months. Our eleven cubic metres of baggage was blocked in Djibouti.

Niskanen's letters appeared in the *Duvbo* yearbook. Significantly perhaps, Mary is hardly mentioned. But his love affair with Ethiopia was about to begin.

His first job, as we have mentioned, was to be a sports instructor for the Imperial Bodyguard cadets. Twice a week he would also go to Debre Zeit, to teach at the airforce headquarters. In 1948, he became a physical education instructor at the Haile Selassie I Secondary School. By 1950, he had been appointed Director of the Physical Education Department at the Ministry of Education. In 1948, he also became part time secretary-general of the Ethiopian Red Cross Society (ECRS), which he was crucial in developing. He was to serve it variously as a member, secretary-general and board member for most of the rest of his life. Niskanen was tireless, and always working in the service of others. He helped set up the All Africa Leprosy & Rehabilitation Training Centre (ALERT), a Red Cross nursing hospital, and he also helped administer and distribute Swedish aid money in what was to become his adopted home. Many of his friends said later that he became more of an Ethiopian than a Swede. He was also to gain respect from people like Prof Rubenson because he came to work "for the Ethiopians, employed by them rather than for and by the Swedish Government or an NGO." Unlike most of the other Swedes, recalls Rubenson, he also "came early and stayed long".

Work, although central to Niskanen's life, was not the be all and end all of it. Besides his contribution to the world of sport, one of the things he is best remembered for is the development of the *Jan Meda* Festival, which was to turn into a major fundraiser for the Red Cross. It was usually held on the great *Jan Meda* field, the training ground of the Imperial Bodyguard, which lay adjacent to their headquarters. Every embassy and country represented in Ethiopia would set up a tent or major stall to sell produce from their country. In the film of one year's festivities, the Dutch tent can be seen surmounted by a seemingly life-size windmill, while the British one is crowned by a great, painted Big Ben. A central attraction at these festivals was the Swedish Folk Dance Team of which Niskanen was, inevitably, chairman and instructor. There are pictures of Niskanen and the troupe in his album. The social cachet of these festivals is underlined by the fact that, at one, the Emperor offered a horse and riding equipment as the tombola's first prize.

As if all of this was not enough, Niskanen made sure he was in the thick of Ethiopia's many crises. He played a role in relief operations when an earthquake disaster hit Kefalo, when Somali troops began an abortive invasion in 1963 and during a drought in the hot and dry region of Sekota. He also worked on various flood and cholera crises. He served as coordinator of Ethiopian-Swedish Red Cross joint services when refugees from southern Sudan flooded into the Gambella district between 1971 and 1973 and helped drought and famine victims in Wollo between 1973 and 1974. In 1963, he found time to fly to Nepal for the Red Cross to investigate the fate of Tibetan refugees and he also went to Kenya in the same year.

But, above all, Niskanen had fun. In a letter to *Duvbo* in 1946, Niskanen wrote that the altitude was interfering with his ability to have a good time. "I tried to dance a smooth tango but felt so weak that I preferred to remain seated for the rest of the evening. The party went on the following night and then I felt stronger." In the early years Niskanen never rested. There were constant parties, visits and excursions. Niskanen and Mary's first house was by the *Jan Meda* field. When it rained the roof leaked, so they moved, together with the horses, dogs and cats that they had acquired, to a stone house with five rooms, a kitchen and servants' cottages.

For the vibrant Swedish community in Ethiopia these were happy days. In fact, for those that lived through them they were the happiest, most exciting times of their lives. Gunvor Ploman is one of them. She went to Addis Ababa in 1946 and became close friends with Niskanen and Mary. They were, she says, her closest friends.

"They were very generous and hospitable. We rode on horseback to all the parties that were given. There were riding excursions to the lowlands every weekend. Beautiful, mystical places. We bathed in the lakes. It was even hotter in the lowlands."

In January 1949, Ragnhild Wahlborg, who had been amongst those so shocked by Mussolini's invasion of Ethiopia, also arrived in Addis Ababa to start work in a hospital. Later she wrote her memoirs, in which she records expeditions arranged by one Richard Nilsson, whom she says was "manager of the Cadet Academy", where Niskanen worked.

> Horseback riding was popular among the Swedish community in those days, and Sunday mornings usually found a company of about 40 or 50, meeting at the Academy, ready for a day's outing. Ethiopian officers and cadets followed us on winding paths through eucalyptus forest until we reached the mountain plateau. There it was "up and away" for anyone who wanted to experience the fascination of speed, wind, open space, sun and blue sky. It was a marvellous feeling of space and freedom that words cannot describe.

Wahlborg seems to have made only one significant omission in her little list.

Ulf Niskanen, Onni's nephew, recalls that every year in September, when his uncle came back to Sweden, he would come into his room every night to tell him about his adventures. "There were hunting stories and plane crashes and they were all true. It was no fantasy." One of the stories was about a hunting expedition undertaken by Niskanen and his best friend at the time, another

Swede called Carl Gustav Forsmark. He worked at Addis Ababa's Technical School. Forsmark went swimming in a river only to be attacked by a baby crocodile which, after a fierce struggle, he managed to stab and kill.

In his letters to *Duvbo*, Niskanen would write colourful accounts of his life. On his first trip with his cadets to Asela, some 175 kilometres south of Addis Ababa, where there was a Swedish hospital and school, they camped, hunted and lived "like Tarzan". Niskanen shot a "jungle bird" that he had stuffed and mounted on his wall. It was to be followed by many other trophies. Hunting was clearly popular among the Swedes and other expatriates in Ethiopia. There was enough work to support a resident Swedish taxidermist and his wife.

One of Niskanen's adventures took place with the local boy scouts whose movement he also found time to set up. He took 102 scouts on a proposed fortnight's camp to Dire Dawa in the west. Somewhere along the line they became stranded in the bush because the railway workers went on strike. The Emperor and his family visited their camp and donated money to pay the increased cost of food. But, the strike went on and the money began to run out. After a month Niskanen used what cash was left to hire two trucks. He packed all the materials and all of the scouts into the vehicles and began the 480 kilometre long trek back to Addis Ababa. The rains had started though and there were 140 rivers to cross, not to mention the journey through malaria infected areas.

Holidays were adventures too. In 1949, he left with Mary for Kilimanjaro in a one-engine plane in bad conditions. He was then forced to make a crash landing in the desert where they nearly died of thirst. Undeterred, Niskanen decided to climb Kilimanjaro along with five British mountaineers, only one of whom made it to the top with him. The holiday was concluded with a week on the island of Zanzibar.

Following another crash Niskanen, travelling this time with Count von Rosen, had to stay with native tribesmen as they fashioned new parts to repair their plane.

In January 1965, Niskanen and his friend Forsmark embarked on a new venture. They helped found and run the gruelling Ethiopian Highland Rally. This was a race around the country, which Niskanen would drive in his red Saab. There is surviving film, which includes clips of Niskanen. It ran annually until 1974 when it fell into abeyance because of the revolution.

At a certain point the Emperor offered Niskanen a piece of land near Nazareth.[2] But Niskanen thought it was not right to accept. He did, however, buy a piece of land near Lake Awasa, south of Addis Ababa, with Forsmark on which they built a petrol station. It was not a success. Some neighbouring Portuguese farmers diverted a river, which flooded the garage, and the money they made when it still worked was filched by a crooked manager. Forsmark later went to India where he died in a rally race.

Later in life, Niskanen began building a house by the lake. Although he had lived abroad for so long, he remained close to his brothers, Arne and Erik, and their plan was to build houses on the same piece of land and retire there with him. The revolution put paid to such dreams.

One of the curious features about Niskanen was the way in which he rigidly divided the parts of his life. The-

---

[2] *Nazareth's original name was Adama. It was renamed Nazareth by Haile Selassie, but in 2000 reverted to Adama.*

re were the sportsmen, of whom more later, his women and his highly active social life. None of these three parts overlapped. Niskanen would spend inordinate amounts of time looking after the sportsmen and caring for them, but they did not feature as friends to be invited to parties or dinners. They were, after all, simple men who could not speak English.

This is not to say, however, that he was not close to them. Still, Wami Biratu knew nothing of Niskanen's personal life at all, not even whether or not he was married. When he sometimes went to Niskanen's house he remembers that "there was a white woman there, I don't know if she was his wife or sister." Hailu Abebe, another runner and contemporary of Bikila and Wami says he knew Niskanen was not married but apart from that:

> We had no idea of his private life. We never talked about personal affairs. In retrospect, yes, it is strange. We knew nothing about him. We regarded him as senior.

Niskanen's social circle embraced the cream of Addis society. Apart from the large Swedish and expatriate communities, including then 15,000 Italians and 5,000 Greeks, it must not be forgotten that Addis Ababa was at that time developing into the cosmopolitan, diplomatic capital of Africa. This was because the nascent Organisation of African Unity found its home here as well as the United Nations' Economic Commission for Africa. Far more exciting for Niskanen though than the short-term diplomats and other foreigners who passed through Addis Ababa was the circle of the Imperial Court.

Over the years Niskanen drew close to the Emperor

and his family. This is underlined by the fact that by the 1960s he had become the star turn at the Emperor's Christmas parties. Every year Haile Selassie would throw a tea party for the children of the royal family, the diplomatic community and other important foreigners. At a certain point Niskanen, dressed as Father Christmas, would appear to distribute the presents. However, the most exciting part of the day was Santa's actual arrival. Tariku Abekira, then a young minor royal, remembers that one year Father Christmas Niskanen descended into the palace grounds by helicopter. In the photo album, there is a picture of Niskanen dressed as Santa accompanied by another Father Christmas. Niskanen was also an accomplished magician and delighted in entertaining children with magic shows.

In the early 1970s, Ulf Niskanen, then 18-years-old, went to visit the uncle he had loved as a child. The idea was that he would stay and work as a volunteer at Addis Ababa's leprosy centre of which Niskanen was now director. But the two quarrelled. Ulf, then in the flush of youthful leftism, was horrified by the poverty, the sight of people dying on the streets – and the wealth of the court. Ulf recalls: "he (Onni) said 'the Emperor has done a lot for this country.'"

In 1972, Onni called his brother Erik and told him that the Crown Princess (the wife of the Emperor's son), had a bad back. He should build a sauna and bring it to Addis Ababa. He did so. After a week of waiting the family was duly summoned for tea at the palace, an experience they have never forgotten.

This visit may well be related to a run-in Niskanen had, at about this time, with Arne Carlsgard, then head of the Swedish equivalent of the Peace Corps in Ethiopia. Niskanen was at this point director of ALERT. One of his young workers was a Swede called Bjorn. Niskanen asked Carlsgard if Bjorn could be taken off the job for ten days or so to build a sauna for the Imperial Family. Carlsgard refused, especially as, by this stage, there was mounting criticism of the Emperor's regime in Sweden. Niskanen was furious and accused Carlsgard of being a petty bureaucrat.

According to ALERT's records, Niskanen earned $1,200 a month at this stage and drove a second hand Mercedes belonging to the organisation. At the time, this was neither a poor wage for a foreigner, nor was it extravagant.

We have another vignette which describes Niskanen's life at the time and his relationship to the court. Haken Landelius was appointed secretary-general of *Radda Barnen* – Swedish Save the Children on 1 September 1972. On the very same day, he received a telegram from the Ethiopian Ministry of Health ordering his organisation in the country to close down. The next day he got on a plane to Addis Ababa and sat next to the Swedish Ambassador to Ethiopia who told him that the only person who could solve his problem was Niskanen. "Onni received me in his beautiful garden," he recalled. "Wherever he lived he created delightful gardens. He was flanked by two big dogs that the Emperor had given him. 'I'll give you the Emperor's telephone number' Onni said to me. 'And I call him just like that?'" Landelius and Niskanen were invited to the palace the very next day:

There were different groups of people standing outside the palace. They were waiting for the Emperor to
come out and settle their disputes like King Solomon.
A man walked by with a lion on a leash. We entered
as the doors were opened by two servants dressed in
traditional Ethiopian coloured robes. The Minister
of Royal Affairs decided to give me the title of "General" saying "Secretary won't do." We stepped into
an enormous room. The Emperor sat on his throne
with the prince next to him. He spoke in Amharic as
it was the only language that could be spoken from
the throne. He had stunning eyes and an incredible
charisma despite his diminutive stature. The Emperor
said: "I know your organisation very well. Let's talk
business." He snapped his fingers and the Minister of
Health crept in. The Emperor ordered reconciliation.
Later I became good friends with the minister, but he
was hanged in 1974.

Several times during his sporting career in Ethiopia,
Niskanen came into conflict with the Ethiopian coaches.
In one dispute, which had gone all the way up to the
Emperor, Selassie ruled in favour of the Swede. "He's
more Ethiopian than you are," he said.

As Niskanen liked to keep his life in neat compart-
ments it is only natural that the one which contains the
information about his private life, his love life, is the one
that is hardest to fathom.

Onni separated from his wife Mary in 1952, but she
stayed on in Addis Ababa for several years, working
as an embassy secretary. They were finally divorced in
November 1956, but seem to have remained on good
terms. Their friend Carmen Rubin, recalling those hea-
dy days many years later in her sunlight-flooded flat in
Stockholm, believes that Niskanen always had so many

things on the go that Mary became lonely. After the separation there were affairs with many women. One was an English woman called Helen Inkpen. Another was a Swede who worked at the Swedish Embassy called Helena. She managed to secure a flat above Niskanen's and when she left she made sure that it did not go to another single woman. In general, the women fell for Niskanen, but not always. He once fell in love with a Swedish doctor called Kristina Tjernstrom, but she was not interested in him.

Niskanen loved parties. His favourite party trick was to chew glass – and swallow it. Nevertheless, many say they never saw Niskanen at a social event with a woman. He was, it seems, extremely discreet. However, there is more to it than that. Fundamentally, women were not high on Niskanen's list of priorities. Sometimes this lead to the mistaken conclusion that he was gay.

Whatever Niskanen's emotions dictated, his attitude to women was often to lead to sorrow. This was certainly the case with the nurse Ragnhild Wahlborg. For years she pined for him and they may well have slept with one another. But this was a classic case of unrequited love. Carmen Rubin says of Ragnhild: "She loved him, but it was not reciprocated."

> It became a deep love but she had no chance. He was not a "one woman man". He wanted to be free. She was very upset about it, but she did not cry because she was a tough woman. She would have liked to marry him. He was the love of her life, but, there was no great love of his life. You never saw him kiss or hug a girl. He wasn't the type.

Later in his life there were rumours that Niskanen was linked romantically with an Ethiopian doctor called Widad Kidane-Mariam. She was glamorous and had an interesting background. She had been born in Jerusalem and studied medicine at the American University in Beirut. She was the first Ethiopian woman ever to become a doctor and was closely involved with Niskanen in the setting up of ALERT. She was certainly a close friend but whether she was a lover too is unknown.

Niskanen's family in Sweden agree that Onni was not very interested in women. That does not mean to say, says May-Elizabet, his sister-in-law, that he did not possess "the Niskanen charm." In his photos that they have at their home there is one of an attractive woman called Annette. They cannot remember her family name. She was Swiss and worked for the Red Cross. In the picture, she is cuddling a cat. On the back, she has written:

24 Oct '54
Which cat do you prefer?

The answer was to be the same as it had been for every woman since Britta Bjork and every woman yet to come. Niskanen liked women – but he liked sport more.

3. The Road to Rome

In March 1961, six months after Bikila's historic victory in Rome, Phil Pilley, the editor of *World Sports*, noted that Onni Niskanen had "moulded" the Ethiopian from a "raw runner" to a "world class competitor". He wrote: "The attack on an Olympic gold medal had been a planned campaign, and, as a result, Niskanen possessed evidence unknown to the world at large: the evidence of his own eyes and his stopwatch." Pilley's observation was truer than he could ever possibly have imagined.

Except for the reference by Michael Lentakis that Niskanen had first spotted Bikila running everyday from Sululta we cannot be sure when the men first met, but it seems likely that they both would have been aware of one another for many years before actually working together. This period began after the Melbourne Olympic games of 1956 which, as Bikila said, had fired his ambition and imagination. Their relationship was clearly well established by 1958 when Niskanen took Bikila to Sweden.

When he first arrived in 1946 to work with the cadets Niskanen began to ready a sports ground a couple of hundred metres from the Emperor's palace. Ragnhild Wahlborg, the nurse, has left us this description of Haile Selassie's residence:

He lived with his family in a house that, according to European standards, was too modest to be called a palace. The Bodyguard band marched by twice a day, creating a festive atmosphere with their splendid uniforms and their precision marching in step with the music. It was an equivalent to our own "Changing of the Guards" and the ever-present crowd of little boys showed great admiration for their performance.

Niskanen believed that his charges were best suited to running and jumping. He also began teaching basketball, handball, football, tennis, swimming, orienteering, riding and gymnastics. "What is the purpose of throwing this thing?" asked one sceptic as Niskanen tried to impart to him the art of discus throwing. From the beginning, he was impressed by his recruits. He wrote later that, "they were fine boys. Easy to teach. Their sporting experience was limited to barefoot soccer. When they kicked the ball and their toes made a cracking noise I could feel it in my own feet."

The Bodyguard recruits made quick progress. When Niskanen arranged the first marathon races through Addis Ababa they were always the winners even if there were competitors from the other services or the police or civilians. Their disadvantage was that they, like the vast majority of potential sportsmen, had no instructors. There were no civil sporting organisations, no clubs, no arenas or sporting facilities, nor were there instructors or managers. From 1950, however, Niskanen had the opportunity to begin to change this, as he was appointed director-general of the Physical Education Department of the Ministry of Education.

Niskanen set about copying the Swedish school sporting structure. With the help of ten physical training instructors from Sweden who were sent out across the country, he began organising the country's sports. Officials were trained, races organised in schools, in the military and the police academies. Niskanen had made, or sent for, a couple of hundred plaques and trophies with which he encouraged competition. He complained though that many did not want to train.

Such was his devotion to the cause that Niskanen spent large amounts of his free time helping coach those who were keen. In this way, he quickly discovered that, in the absence of sports grounds and equipment, long distance running was the natural sport for young Ethiopians. He had also noticed that running was the only way for many ordinary people to get from one place to another. He said later: "Many workers lived several miles from Addis. You could see them jog over the mountains on Friday night to reach their home village and on Monday morning they appeared again, this time carrying a package of food."

By studying his CV, which was left amongst his papers, it is easy to see how Niskanen, from a very early stage, began not only to create a sports infrastructure in Ethiopia but also to forge the crucial Olympic link. In 1948, only two years after he had arrived in the country, Niskanen was present at the London Olympics as an "Ethiopian Observer". The country was not yet represented, even though Haile Selassie had attended the Paris games as far back as 1924. The year of the London games was also crucial because it saw the creation of the forerunner of the Ethiopian Olympic Committee, the first in black Africa. A national committee is a prerequisite to participation in the Olympics. In 1952, at the Helsinki games, Niskanen was also an observer. He carefully kept his press pass as a souvenir, which shows that he was accredited as a journalist for the English language paper, the *Ethiopian Herald*.

The visit to Helsinki must have been an emotional moment for Niskanen. It was, after all, here that his past and future came together. Exactly eight years before he had just escaped death in the service of Finland. Now he was back, but in the service of his new love - Ethiopia. It also seems possible, though Niskanen's CV is unclear about the date, that it was here that he introduced the country as a membership candidate to the International Olympic Committee. The ambitious Niskanen knew exactly what he was doing. Exactly eight years later all his work was to bear fruit as Bikila stormed to victory in Rome.

Of course times had changed since Haile Selassie had been at the Paris games in 1924, but still Niskanen had helped do something which the Emperor had long dreamed of. There he had discussed Ethiopia's participation in the Olympic movement with Baron Pierre de Coubertin, the founder of the modern Olympics and then still the president of the International Olympic Movement. However, his successor, the Belgian Count Henri de Baillet-Latour was less sympathetic and so Ethiopia's request to participate in the Amsterdam games of 1928 fell on stony ground.

Back in Addis Ababa, Niskanen, apart from his work, was engaged in several projects. Between 1948 and 1954, he was a member of the Ethiopian Football Federation. The young Bikila was mainly interested in football, and so, even if he saw him running, it seems quite possible that Niskanen saw him playing football in this period too.

In 1954, Niskanen was chairman of a five-man committee of Swedes in Ethiopia who were asked to look into the question of how best to disburse Swedish aid money. Niskanen wanted to set up a physical training school on the Swedish model but eventually it was decided to establish a joint Ethiopian-Swedish Building College instead. Perhaps disappointed by this decision, Niskanen returned home. For the next two years, he studied at the Royal Swedish Physical Education Institute where he brushed up his skills and technique. While he was there, two Ethiopians were also studying at the institute. One, Belete Ergetie, we shall meet again later.

When he returned in 1956, Niskanen helped train the first Ethiopian athletes ever to go to the Olympic games. That year they were held in Melbourne. Among them was the runner Mamo Wolde. At the same time, he was back again as director of physical education at the Ministry of Education – and part time secretary-general of the Ethiopian Red Cross.

Niskanen did not go to Melbourne because he had to return to Sweden to complete his annual period of military service, which he was due to serve in his capacity as a reserve officer. Another Swede, Bertil Larsson, went in his stead. For the Ethiopians, the Melbourne games were not a success. Sergeant Bashaye Feleke took part in the marathon and came 29th out of 48 contestants while Gebre Birkay came 32nd. The Ethiopians won no medals. Memorable, however, was the problem the team faced when presented with a baby kangaroo which was a gift for the Emperor - and a major headache to fly home.

Niskanen and Bikila began to get to know each other properly, and work together, in the years 1956-58. This was the period in which Bikila was beginning to distinguish himself. In 1956, soon after he had taken up running properly, he had already come second to Wami Biratu, the reigning marathon champion in the annual Armed Forces championships. By 1958, the bond was already close. Niskanen returned to Sweden in the September of that year with three Ethiopians. They were Bikila, Mamo Wolde and a third, now forgotten, called Said Mussa. At first, they stayed in his brother Erik's house. They then moved to a training college at Boson, outside Stockholm. Onni told his family that these Ethiopians were destined to be the great runners of the future.

The Niskanens remember that Onni spoke Amharic to the Ethiopians, who were rather quiet but "very nice". The atmosphere was relaxed. For fun, Ulf, Niskanen's nephew, then six or seven-years-old, ran around the track at Boson in competition with Bikila. By the time he had made it around once Bikila had streaked past four times! The runner then got sick eating raw meat, which as *kitfo*, the Ethiopian equivalent of steak tartare, is a staple part of Ethiopian cuisine. When he hurt his toe, Erik looked after it.

It has often been said that Bikila's place at the Olympics in Rome was not assured until just before the team left. However, the fact that Niskanen had picked him out to take to Sweden to train for a month or so in 1958 implies exactly what Pilley had written, that is to say that the "attack" on the Olympic gold had been a long planned operation. More than that, we know quite a lot about their training.

From various accounts we have quite detailed notes about the type of training Niskanen prescribed for his athletes. From 1964, just before the Tokyo Olympics, we have this eyewitness account of Bikila and Mamo Wolde from *World Sports* magazine:

> They are preparing themselves by pitting their stamina and strength against the back-breaking hills in the heat and the rarefied atmosphere of the Ethiopian highlands.
>
> As these two wiry athletes jog their way through lush green fields in the foothills of Ethiopia's 3,650m Entoto Mountains, their arms working like pistons, their feet pounding the red earth in unison, the tin roofs of Addis Ababa, capital of this 3,000-year-old land of the Queen of Sheba, glint far below in the searing sun.
>
> The runners pass farmers driving teams of oxen, ploughing the land in much the same way as their forefathers did in biblical times.

Tsige Abebe writes that the following was a typical week's schedule prepared for her father by Niskanen. She says that it began with gym routines and varied by the day:

Monday:
Morning: 30 kilometres out of city – Sululta.
Tuesday:
Morning: 10 kilometres medium speed, stadium.
Afternoon: 15 kilometres medium speed, paved roads.

Wednesday:
Morning: Up and down hill relays.
Afternoon: 15 kilometres fast speed, paved roads.
Thursday:
Morning: Stadium tracks, relays– 5 x 400 metres,
10 x 800 metres, 5 x 1000 metres with a 200 metre
interval per heat.
Afternoon: 30 kilometres medium speed, paved
roads.
Friday:
Morning: 50 kilometres, first half at fast speed and
second at medium.
Saturday: Competition in half marathon
Sunday: Break.

Her father, she writes, would also take himself off, even
on a Sunday, training, on Mount Entoto and elsewhere.
Often while training Niskanen would follow his charge
in a car encouraging him and handing out drinks. For a
serious Olympic-targeted athlete this schedule might be
relatively normal except for Friday's 50 kilometre run
which seems excessive. Oddly, Niskanen himself wrote
the following contradictory account about training: "I
give prominence to quality over quantity. I believe 10 kilometres is a more suitable distance than 30 kilometres.
They are used to run 10 kilometres. But every fortnight
they will do 20 kilometres as a test."

He also emphasised the importance of a relaxed running style. He said that Bikila did not have inherent talent
and had to put a lot of work into his technique: "When I
started training him he ran like a drilling soldier. A long
distance runner must concentrate on running with a mi-
nimum loss of energy." Perhaps the contradiction about

distances may reflect changes in his ideas over time. Niskanen also understood that being a coach meant more than taking care of runners in training. "The coach has to understand the adept's temperament, family conditions and interests," he wrote.

> When the coach has achieved this, to get the adept motivated he has to lay out a program full of variety. Strength, stamina and speed must be stimulated as well as the mind ... Every time an athlete starts a race he must have a realistic goal. When he succeeds he will gain self-confidence. So the coach ought rather to play down expectations rather than exaggerate them.

Robert Parienté, the veteran French sports journalist who worked for *L'Equipe* and who has written extensively about marathon running, says that Niskanen's ideas about coaching were formed in the 1930s. They had come from the so-called Swedish "Natural School" whose notions were developed by Gosta Olander. A trainer, cinematographer and mountain guide, Olander's ideas derived from studying the movement of animals in Valadalen, deep in rural central Sweden where he lived. Olander was the trainer of Gunder Hagg, Sweden's record breaking, champion middle distance runner of the 1940s. Olander encouraged running on "supple terrain" that is to say not on roads but earth, and he was in the avant-garde of training methods because he had studied the difference between "endurance" and "stamina".

Alain Lunzenfichter, also of *L'Equipe* and one of the world's most respected writers on both the Olympics and marathons, says that to understand the latter it is important to divide the race into two parts. The first 30 kilometres are the "prologue" which is the period where "stamina" is needed. This is defined as the ability to keep up a high speed for a long period of time. It is something that the sprinter does not have, it has to be worked at and it can increase over the years. The trick then is to arrive at the 30 kilometre point without being exhausted. The last 12 kilometres are the "monologue", also called the period of "endurance". This is defined as the ability not so much to keep up a high speed, but rather the ability to keep going. According to Lunzenfichter, Bikila's genius was his capacity for "extreme endurance", of being able to keep fresh, "to run on endurance the whole way." Niskanen's role then was to "bring Scandinavian rigour to a people who had much more sporting qualities than they did."

According to Parienté, Niskanen discovered in Ethiopia athletes naturally endowed with both "stamina" and "endurance", that is to say attributes which did not have to be acquired through training. As we have seen, though, Niskanen would at least in part have disagreed with this, since he thought that Bikila's talents were *not* inherent. Nevertheless in Parienté's view:

> Niskanen was a man who discovered a goldmine. He was a kind of explorer. He modified the way Bikila ran – making him run faster in a natural environment, not in a stadium but with lots of ups and downs. He cultivated his "stamina".

Parienté also notes that Rhadi Ben Abdesselem, the Moroccan who came second to Bikila in Rome had the same attributes and, like Bikila, had spent his youth as a shepherd at high altitude, in his case the Rif Mountains. "He was in the French Army and his officers noticed that he never got tired. So, he had 'endurance'. They began to train him to develop his "stamina."

We now know that one of the reasons why Ethiopians, East Africans and others, like Rhadi, are naturally gifted in marathon running is because they come from areas of high altitude. In the 1960s, partly thanks to the success of Bikila and others, this was only just beginning to be understood. At its most basic level the explanation relates to the way that haemoglobin, the oxygen-containing protein in red blood cells works slightly differently in people who come from high altitudes, enabling them to breathe better while running. So, according to Lunzenfichter: "Running 120 kilometres at 2,000 metres altitude is the equivalent of running 300 kilometres at lower levels."

Training sessions with Niskanen might well end with a massage and sauna. The first sauna in Ethiopia was built by a Swedish couple called Arne and Carmen Rubin. Niskanen would bring the athletes to their house, but when the Rubins left in 1962 Niskanen bought their sauna and had it installed in his own house.

The sauna, while relaxing, would have had very little, if any, beneficial effect on the capacities of the athletes. However, Niskanen would also take care to prepare special foods for them. Roman Reta, Niskanen's cook, says that his master prepared their food and drinks himself. Rose-hip soup and pollen were two undistinguished Swedish ingredients of Niskanen's success formula. This soup is a traditional Swedish recipe often served as a dessert. It is high in Vitamin C, a thirst quencher if served

Bikila seconds from winning the marathon, Rome 1960. (New York Times)

Abebe Bikila, left, and Rhadi Ben Abdesselem, immediately after the marathon, Rome 1960. (AFP-Getty Images)

Bikila, victorious. Rome, 1960. (Niskanen collection)

Bikila sports his gold medal. Rhadi Ben Abdesselem of Morocco, left, won silver and Barry Magee of New Zealand won the bronze. Rome 1960. (Getty Images)

Return from Rome. The Emperor decorates Bikila. On Bikila's right is General Merid Mengesha, minister of defence and president of the Ethiopian Sports Confederation. (Tadele Yidenekatchew collection)

After his victory Bikila toured the country. Here he is being introduced by Yidnekatchew Tessema, who led the Ethiopian teams to the Rome, Tokyo and Mexico Olympics. (Tadele Yidnekatchew collection)

Onni Niskanen in Finnish uniform.
(Niskanen collection)

Bikila in the uniform of the Imperial
Bodyguard. (Niskanen collection)

Bikila and the mascot of the Imperial Bodyguard. (Niskanen collection)

Trainer and runner share a joke. Niskanen and Bikila together.
(Niskanen collection)

The Empress Menen, Haile Selassie and Niskanen.
(Ulf Niskanen, private collection)

Niskanen washes the feet of the champion.
(Niskanen collection)

Bikila and Mamo Wolde. Boston marathon,
April 1963. (Time & Life Pictures – Getty Images)

Bikila adored. (Niskanen collection)

Bikila in training. (Niskanen collection)

chilled, and is often used as a remedy for colds. Initially, Bikila was not overly keen on such foreign concoctions. He preferred traditional Ethiopian food and according to his daughter, "did not have any special diet for his running":

> He had three meals a day whenever possible. Fried eggs and a glass of milk for breakfast. On fasting days, he used to take barley porridge or fruits and tea in place of milk. For lunch and supper, he had 'Injera' with stew prepared from sheep meat or 'Doro Wat' (Chicken Stew) as available, and he loved them prepared in the traditional way, with a heavy component of chilli powder and butter. It did not make any difference to him if he dined on meals with a large dosage of fat, he usually burned or used it up during his hard training.
>
> He paid less attention to the advice of Niskanen who used to discourage him against eating too much fat and chilli. His favourite dish was meat and he used to enjoy it in all forms. Occasionally, he dined on raw steak with lots of chilli powder in it.

Being religious, Bikila observed the "fasting days" of the Ethiopian Orthodox Church. This meant not eating meat on Wednesdays and Fridays nor during other prescribed periods. The runner was also keen on his afternoon siesta.

There is little doubt that Niskanen's relationships with his athletes were close. There is also no doubt that his relationship with Bikila was the closest of all. There was, however, a language barrier. At first Bikila spoke no English, although later he learned a little. Niskanen spoke some Amharic but it always remained somewhat basic. Nevertheless, everyone who knew them confirms that they were close. Carmen Rubin, Niskanen's friend, remembers that "Onni cared for Bikila like a baby, taking care of his massages, food, sleep. Every little thing. They were as close as they could be under the circumstances. Bikila was like a very simple little boy. He had not seen the world. He was very polite, very humble. From the bottom of his heart he was a good man."

Belete Ergetie, one of the two Ethiopians who had been at college in Stockholm at the same time as Niskanen, says: "They were close friends because during that time Abebe Bikila needed Niskanen's presence for his success. Niskanen brought herb teas and glucose and things for Bikila while he was in Sweden." Later Belete was to marry a Swede and retire to Sweden.

Tsige Abebe says that Niskanen used to say that Bikila was his "only son" and many believe that the relationship was similar to that of a father and son. The more cynical see a master-servant type relationship. This is perhaps because of the rigid divisions Niskanen made in his life. That is to say that his social life, his love life and his life with the athletes never overlapped. But, Niskanen knew that the athletes would not have liked to mix with his other friends. They inhabited utterly different worlds. The runners were, after all, simple men who would have felt intimidated by their trainer's urbane, educated and often aristocratic Ethiopian friends, not to mention his European ones. They had nothing in common with them.

Interestingly, all Niskanen's friends and family say, like Carmen Rubin, that Bikila was quiet and humble. In fact, it seems that, partly because of the language problem, this was how he reacted with Europeans. With

Ethiopians from the same background as himself he was a completely different character and far more self-assertive – but of this more later.

Another point is that the relationship between Niskanen and Bikila did not stay the same from beginning to end. It changed over time. There is little doubt that before Rome it was perhaps more impersonal and business-like than it became afterwards. Until 1960, Niskanen had been concentrating on creating the perfect runner, making of Bikila and the other Ethiopians the champion athlete that he had always wanted to be in his own youth. Then, from 1960 to 1964, the nature of their friendship changed. Niskanen, as Carmen Rubin observed, took care of Bikila's every little need. After 1964, things slowly changed again. Bikila grew up. He also became arrogant and gradually began to grow away from the man who had made him.

Knowing that Niskanen had brought Bikila to Sweden in 1958 means it is clear that he had already recognised him and Mamo Wolde (who had, of course, been in Melbourne in 1956, as the champions of the future. However, to other Ethiopians this didn't become clear until July 1960. During the Armed Forces championships Bikila beat Wami Biratu, until then Ethiopia's fastest marathon runner, in a time of 2 hours 39 minutes 50 seconds. This competition was very prestigious and held annually in the presence of the Emperor. In 1952, Emil Zatopek's record-smashing Helsinki Olympic marathon time had been 2 hours 23 minutes 0.3 seconds. Bikila was nowhere near this *yet* but he was getting there.

Three to four months before the Rome Olympics were due to start, the Ethiopian sporting authorities made arrangements for prospective candidates for the games and their trainers to go to the air force base at Debre Zeit to train. Not only were there all the proper facilities there, including good beds and food, but it was also deemed better for the athletes since it was 1,000 metres lower than Addis Ababa. A black American trainer was brought in for this period to advise and the basic work was done by five Ethiopian coaches and Niskanen. Because of their good times, the lack of money and the failure of the 1956 Melbourne team to win anything, it was decided to concentrate on the long-distance runners. According to Belete Ergetie, who was there as a potential candidate: "Bikila had good training results, he was very very determined and we were focusing on him." He adds: "For most of the time he was looked after by Onni Niskanen."

At Debre Zeit tension began to rise and there was intrigue amongst the athletes. Ergetie recalls that some of them played tricks to put the others off. These included putting dead rats in other peoples' beds.

There were four star marathon runners but there were only going to be two places for Rome. The stars were Wami Biratu, Abebe Wakjira, who was in the army but not a Guardsman, a policeman whose name no one can remember, and Bikila. In the middle of the training the policeman disappeared. Many reckoned that Biratu and Wakjira would be selected. The final heats began – with some fifty or more runners taking part. Biratu led but suddenly had to drop out. He had been afflicted with boils. Bikila streaked to victory recording a time of 2 hours 21 minutes 23 seconds. Niskanen and the others were astounded – and ecstatic. Not only had Bikila sliced

18 minutes off his time since the Armed Forces contest of a few weeks before but he had just pulverised Zatopek's record too.

Wakjira came in second with a personal best of 2 hours 30 minutes 26 seconds. Both were selected but Niskanen wrote later that he had had to fight for the 39-year-old Wakjira who, some argued, was not good enough for Rome.

Over the next few days they were prepared for the trip. They were issued with two suits each and given $150 in pocket money. Before they left they gave $50 each to their families. The athletes were then taken to meet the Emperor. They lined up just outside the palace where they were to be introduced by Yidnekatchew Tessema, the leader of the Ethiopian delegation. Abebe Wakjira, who in 1997 was 77-years-old and living in relative poverty in the little provincial town of Fiche, some two hours drive north of Addis Ababa, remembers the scene vividly:

> The Emperor asked who was who and then he saw us. Both of us were very thin and he said: "Who are they?" Yidnekatchew said we were the marathon runners and he replied: "How can such thin people win?" Yidnekatchew then told the Emperor our times but he replied: "I didn't ask you for their times I asked you whether they could win or not!" Yidnekatchew did not reply.

The Emperor appears to have been mildly amused by this but was certainly not amused to discover that the athletes were leaving for Rome the next day – and he had not been informed. All the while the Emperor's little dog had been sniffing and rooting about at the athletes' feet.

For Yidnekatchew and Niskanen the run up to the Olympics had proved to be a trying time. One of the main problems was money. Because the Ethiopian team in Melbourne in 1956 had failed to win anything there was a strong lobby which argued against sending a team to Rome. Niskanen was important in persuading the powers that be that Ethiopia should be represented. Yidnekatchew too argued powerfully that, since the Ethiopians had been in Melbourne, if they now did not go to Rome, this would be interpreted as "unhealed ill feelings" left over from the invasion and that it was thus particularly important to go to help normalise the relations between the two countries.

The next problem lay in rivalry between the Army and the Bodyguard, the commanders of the latter at first refusing to let their men participate in the Olympic trials. Niskanen intervened appealing to Colonel Bekele Gezaw, who was then chief of sports in the Army and later of the Bodyguard itself. He asked him to let Bodyguard hopefuls participate in Army trials. In this way, Bikila had begun to emerge. However, Niskanen's troubles were far from over. The problem was that Ethiopian coaches now began to lobby hard against him - or at least that is one version of the story.

In this version of the tale they wanted one of their own to go to Rome. Niskanen, however, had plenty of plus points on his side. Not only had he prepared the marathon runners who wanted him to go but he was also a trained masseur – and this skill could be used to the benefit of the whole team. He also had experience of international sporting events, a year's medical training and could help out with general administration matters. Still the Ethiopian coaches protested bitterly about his inclusion and, if they could not knock Niskanen out of the delegation, they made one last effort to have an Ethiopian coach included as an assistant. This plan collapsed a few days before the departure of the team because, to save money, the Council of Ministers decided not to include the boxers and to cut the size of the contingent from 30 to 15. Yidnekatchew now began to worry, because if the results from Rome were bad he, as an ally of Niskanen, would be in serious trouble. Also, no funds would be forthcoming for international sporting events in future.

Colonel Bekele Gezaw remembers this bitter quarrel well, saying that it had to be resolved by the Emperor himself. Bekele appealed, on Niskanen's behalf, to Lieutenant General Merid Mengesha, the minster of defence and president of the Ethiopian Sports Confederation, who took the matter to the palace. The Emperor agreed that Niskanen should go to Rome and that was the end of the matter.

The other version of the story comes from Belete Ergetie, who was a professional coach but had also been at Debre Zeit as a potential Olympic candidate for the relay team, which had not made the grade. According to him, one of the Ethiopian coaches, Lakew Yigletu, was selected by a vote of the Ethiopian coaches to go to Rome but he was vetoed by Yidnekatchew who did not like him. Ergetie himself was then chosen in his stead. He says that he then turned down the chance to go to Rome because he had not been at Debre Zeit working as a coach and thought it unfair to the others that had.

They then voted again and, somewhat to his surprise, Niskanen was chosen.

With the quarrels over, the team was ready to leave. Bikila had, of course, already been on an aeroplane when he had been to Sweden in 1958. Wakjira had not. Asked whether he was nervous when he boarded a plane for the first time he said "no" because he was "a soldier". He did remember that he and Bikila "were nervous about the shoes though."

4. Roman Triumph

The Rome Olympics were spectacular and well organised. They began on Thursday, August 25th and all the
city's church bells were rung in celebration. One hundred thousand people jammed the Stadio Olimpico to
witness the opening celebrations. Even the hard-nosed
journalists who later wrote their accounts of the day
were impressed. In the minds of the Italian organisers
the games were meant to mark the country's post-war
renaissance and in this they were a brilliant success. The
Italian economy was booming and Rome itself was the
living symbol of *La Dolce Vita*, Federico Fellini's iconic
film of the same year.

Donato Martucci was the press chief of the Italian
Olympic Committee for the games of 1960. He recalls:
"We wanted to show that we were a free country, a new
progressive nation, one that had left fascism behind."
Martucci also remembers that the Rome Olympics were
the last before the games were "taken over" by commer-
cial sponsors.

In preparation for the games, huge construction projects had been undertaken. The Stadio Olimpico was
built next to Mussolini's old stadium, which is still, spec-
tacularly, surrounded by scores of male nude statues. A

seedy area populated by Roma (gypsies), refugees and in Martucci's words "thieves" was cleared away to build the Olympic village and several other sports facilities. Hundreds of volunteers were recruited to help run the show and welcome visitors.

Giacomo Mazzocchi, then a young sports fan, who was later to work for the International Amateur Athletics Federation (IAAF), has fond memories of the games and recalls the relaxed atmosphere. Unlike those that followed this was to be the last Olympics where it was possible for members of the public to mix with the athletes and to go and watch them training.

In his *Olympic Diary: Rome 1960*, Neil Allen, a British sports journalist who was to cover successive games notes:

> The upper class Romans, at first *blasé* about the Olympics, had now decided that it was the chic thing to attend the opening ceremony. So the smart set, the men always fascinated by their own clothes, the women always immensely proud of their own tan, were jostled about until they got to the comparative safety of their own seats.

With three salvoes of guns the games began. Doves went "wheeling round the stadium and into the sky" and the bells "pealed out their song". Allen added: "Full marks to the Italians!"

There was no question of any *blasé* attitudes affecting the Ethiopian team. Niskanen and Yidnekatchew kept their charges on a tight leash. They were allowed to watch some of the events including most of the athletics and they toured some of the sights in a special Olympic tour bus which had been laid on. For most of the time Niskanen was with the athletes. They were sent to bed early and there was absolutely no question of their sampling the Roman nightlife. With their pocket money they went out to do some shopping and bought tee shirts and (ordinary) shoes. When they got lost they stopped people in the street, showed them their Olympic badges on their jackets and according to Wakjira, "People were very friendly, they took us back to the Olympic village." Sometimes there was some limited good-humoured banter about Italy, Ethiopia and the past.

As for Niskanen himself, Rome provided an opportunity for him to catch up with his family. His brother Arne had come to meet him.

There was also training to do. Niskanen took the marathon runners along the course but apparently they did not run it before the day. There now came the question of the shoes. Generally they did not run with shoes but there was, hovering in the background, the question of national prestige. If they ran without shoes it might seem as though the Ethiopians were too poor to afford them. Bikila and Wakjira ran a 10 kilometre trial with shoes to test them out. They hurt their feet and slowed them down. After consulting with Niskanen it was decided that they would not wear them. There is a story that Bikila began the race with shoes and then took them off. This is not what Wakjira remembers. In fact, he says that just before the race began he and Bikila hid in the tent because people were laughing at the two barefoot Ethiopians.

Thanks to the brilliant film made of the Rome marathon we can fill in many details that would otherwise have been lost. As the athletes begin the race it is possible to see that Bikila and Wakjira did indeed start the race without shoes. In Tsige Abebe's book there is this account:

> The sneakers he brought with him were worn out, so they had to go shopping for sneakers suited to the purpose. He wore the new sneakers around for a few days before the competition started in order to break them in. However his pointed, slender feet could not adapt to the sneakers; instead his feet developed painful blisters. This naturally made him worry as to how he was going to go through 42 kilometres of race. No solution seemed to be in sight. He considered the matter at length, and there was only one thing to do, run barefoot ... To Niskanen who had promised victory for Ethiopia, the fact of Abebe's running barefoot only struck him as inviting defeat.

Just before the race, Rhadi Ben Abdesselem of Morocco managed, by chance, to steal a good look at Bikila's feet. His account differs from Tsige's "slender" version. It was published in an athletics magazine and then cited in a book written by Alain Lunzenfichter on the marathon: Rhadi recalls meeting Bikila on the morning of the marathon because an Italian doctor had asked them both to come. When he got there Bikila was already there stretched out on the bed.

> I was amazed by his feet. I knew later that he ran barefoot. The soles of his feet were as thick and black as coal. I remember that I wanted to touch his feet, the hard skin of which resembled, by its consistency, the tyres of big military trucks. I was sure that he would feel nothing, but on the contrary. This hard skin was

very sensitive: I hardly brushed it with my finger and he jumped up on the bed and gave me an astounded look.

Tsige Abebe also notes that, just before the race, a journalist, speaking through a translator asked Bikila why he chose to run barefoot. He replied that it was habit. He then asked him if he thought he would finish the race to which Bikila replied tartly: "If I were not going to finish the race, I wouldn't start it to begin with."

Meanwhile tensions had been rising in the Ethiopian camp. Normally the marathon takes place at some point in the middle of the games but this time the Italians had fixed the event for the end. The problem was that, until then, the Ethiopian team had done badly; the cyclist, Geremew Demoba, had fallen during a race and broken his shoulder. Knives were already being drawn in Addis Ababa. Yidnekatchew Tessema, who was leading the delegation, recalled later that the authorities, or rather those who had opposed sending the team in the first place, were feeling vindicated. "Why squander so much money?" they had asked. "These rumours were a cause of great concern and worry among members of the delegation. The only hope left for us was Abebe Bikila."

The race began at 5.30 in the afternoon of Saturday, September 10th. The weather was good, the sun shining and the sky brilliantly blue. The athletes gathered on Michelangelo's sublime Piazza del Campidoglio, the statue of Emperor Marcus Aurelius looking down on them. They then made their way down to the foot of the Cordonata, its great stairway, to where the race was due to begin. Bikila and Wakjira were wearing orange shorts and green shirts. Bikila's was emblazoned with 11, his number. They went unnoticed, especially as, being unknowns, they had not been ranked in the top 20 hopefuls by the experts. Harald Lechenperg, an Austrian journalist and photographer, noted that, "even if there had been half a dozen Abebes, no one would have paid particular attention. The Swedish trainer has said that they are first-class runners, but for most onlookers they are just two men with tongue-twisting names."

In fact, Niskanen had revealed Bikila's time of 2 hours 21 minutes 23 seconds which he had clocked up in the final Olympic trials. No one took it seriously though, many believing that there must have been something wrong with Niskanen's stopwatch.

The favourite amongst the 69 runners was a Russian called Sergei Popov. He had won the European title in Stockholm in 1958 with a breathtaking world best time of 2 hours 15 minutes 17 seconds. Highly rated, too, was Rhadi Ben Abdesselem, the Moroccan who had seen Bikila's feet. Until now, he had competed under the French flag but Morocco had just become independent and so he was competing under its banner. Rhadi was still, however, in the French army. He was a French and international cross-country champion. He was unsure of his age but thought he was 31-years-old.

Just before the race began the athletes limbered up, did exercises and jogging to get ready. On the Olympic film Bikila can be seen wearing a blue tracksuit. As the athletes gathered, ready for the off, thousands crowded to get a glimpse of them. Popov, hammer and sickle emblazoned on his shirt, was confident, laughing and joking with a friend. For a second the camera caught Bikila's face. He looked extremely tense. The commentary asks: "And what's this Ethiopian called?"

The course was the regulation 42.195 kilometres long and was selected to be the most spectacular marathon of all. One journalist described it as an "athletic opera". From the bottom of the steps of the Campidoglio, the athletes were to swing past the vast wedding cake of the Victor Emmanuel monument, which had been finished in 1935, round down the Via dei Fori Imperiali, the Roman Forum, which is to say the very heart of ancient Rome, past the Colosseum, the Arch of Constantine and then up past the vast ruins of the Baths of Caracalla. The course then took them out through parts of modern Rome before striking for home along the Via Appia Antica, begun by Appius Claudius in the year 312 BC.

Before the race began Niskanen advised his men whom to watch out for and to memorise their numbers. They were the Russians, Rhadi, Barry Magee from Ireland and a couple of others. To encourage them he also told them that he was sure they would be in the top ten. Niskanen's advice was to lead to some confusion though because although Rhadi had been entered as 26, he in fact ran as 185. This was because he was still wearing the number he had worn during the 10,000 metres race two days before. Later Niskanen claimed that because of this Bikila had not realised that his opponent was Rhadi and that if he had he "would have gone on the attack much earlier and would probably have cut two minutes off his time."

On the shot the athletes were off. But, as they left there was commotion. The *New York Times* reported that: "There was a mob scene at the starting point, at the foot of the stairs, with thousands of onlookers jamming the road and cars and buses trying to get through." It took "frantic exertions" says the paper by Lord Burghley, a member of the International Olympic Committee, and other members of the committee to "get the crowd pushed back so the runners would have enough room. The police were not much help." Lord Burghley's association with the Olympics went back a long way. He had competed in 1924 in Paris, the games at which Haile Selassie had been present and won the 440 metres in 1928.

In the film Wakjira – 12 – can be seen just ahead of Bikila. After the initial crush, the numbers of spectators began to thin out but there was a constant line along the whole course. Spectators can even be seen perched on the great walls of the Colosseum, cheering the runners on in groups.

Bikila was not amongst the leaders at the very beginning. Soon, however, groups began to detach themselves. Bikila was in the second along with Popov and Magee. By the fifth kilometre Bikila was towards the back of the first group of five. They consisted of Rhadi, the Englishman Arthur Keily, the Belgian Aurele Vandendriessche and Allal Saoudi, another Moroccan.

By the 15th kilometre the leading group was down to four, Saoudi had dropped away. The film cameraman racing along in a vehicle beside the runners was beginning to take notice of Bikila. He was focusing on his feet. "The little Abyssinian … races along with his thin, sinewy legs like some long-distance runner of Biblical times, nimble as a deer," wrote Lechenperg. At the 18th kilometre the final duel began. Rhadi shot ahead with Bikila powering behind him. From now to the end the race was between these two men alone. "The two run in rhythm like a four-legged tandem," said Lechenperg. Because of the above-mentioned confusion over numbers, Bikila had not realised that he was running with Rhadi. There were three Moroccans in the race and Niskanen wrote later that Bikila:

> ... thought it was one of the other Moroccans that was keeping up with him and expected Rhadi to turn up ahead. Therefore he saved his strength during the last five kilometres and didn't run faster than necessary. He was prepared to put in an extra effort if the Moroccan favourite, Rhadi, turned up.

At the 30th kilometre, as they entered the Via Appia, Bikila began to nudge ahead - but barely. Night was falling. Lechenperg's description is amongst the most dramatic:

> The little moustachioed, brown-skinned man is running so lightly that his feet scarcely seem to touch the ground. Most of the competitors have taken some refreshment meanwhile at a snack-bar beside the course which purveys blueberry juice, glucose and similar fortifiers. But Abebe refuses any nourishment. He is used to running, thirsty or not ... Meanwhile dusk has fallen. The course now runs along the Via Appia ... Along this stretch of road there is a *bersagliere* soldier posted at every ten yards with a flaming torch in his hand to light the way. The scene is a fantastic one, and seems almost unearthly as the silhouettes of the marathon runners flash by.
>
> The wheels of time seem to have been turned back by twenty centuries. Dimly the runners can discern old memorials with weathered inscriptions, fragments of ancient walls, carved gravestones and headless statues. But they can spare no thoughts for these, for they must

summon the last resources of their bodily energy ...
The Via Appia Antica is lined with dense crowds on
either side. Women are to be seen kneeling and cros-
sing themselves as the runners flit past, wraith-like.

At 39.3 kilometres they passed the church of *Domi-
ne Quo Vadis* where St Peter is said to have met Christ
while fleeing from Rome. Minutes later, they came to
the fourth century Ethiopian obelisk of Axum, looted by
Mussolini's soldiers a quarter of a century before. Axum
had been the capital of one of the great early Ethiopian
empires and Mussolini had had the 24 metre high stele
erected in front of his Ministry of Italian East Africa with
some fanfare. After the war, this building, from where
Ethiopia had been run by the Italians, was handed over
to the UN's Food and Agriculture Organisation. It is
possible, and indeed widely believed, that Niskanen told
Bikila that when he saw the obelisk, which was exactly
two kilometres from the finish, he was to break into his
final sprint. Writing later Niskanen records that Bikila
did indeed begin to sprint at this point, but does not
say whether he had told him to or not. Wakjira does
not even remember passing the stele, saying only that
he was concentrating on the running. True or not, Bikila began to pull ahead. By the 41st kilometre Bikila
was five metres ahead. Rhadi could no longer catch him.
Alain Lunzenfichter, the author of *Le Roman de Marathon* and a marathon runner himself says: "You must
understand just how psychologically crushing it is when
you are passed."

Although Bikila was now sprinting the last 2,000 metres or so to the finish, in the stretch before that he had
not been faster than everyone else, but had rather slowed

down less than everyone else. Where he had sped up and left everyone else but Rhadi behind was somewhere around the 20 kilometre mark. Niskanen wrote later that: "Abebe was told to take it relatively easy during the first 20 kilometres ... and it is clear that he really did follow instructions." Then he added: "Most of the favourites lagged more and more behind due to the high speed between 20 and 30 kilometres, and Rhadi was the only one who continued to keep up, but even for him the speed remained too high, which showed when he let go when Abebe Bikila put in a sprint in the last kilometre."

For the last stretch of the race, stands had been erected but many seats were actually empty, although thousands were standing. The *New York Times* speculated that they were after a cheaper view. "Thousands of others were gathered beyond the Arch of Constantine," wrote correspondent Allison Danzig, "They could not see anything, but they wanted to be near the spectacular setting for the finish. The police had a job to keep them behind the barriers when the cheering began for the first runner to come into sight, Bikila."

With a thousand metres to go panic set in in the press box. Bikila was speeding to victory now but none of the journalists had ever heard of him. Allen wrote:

> Suddenly we could see the lights of a little convoy twinkling in the distance, nearer came the cars, there was a brief tussle with one of the persistent Lambretta scooters before it was bundled away and then – here he came ... trotting rhythmically and strongly up the Appian Way, the route of the conquerors in a city where his ancestors had once been slaves.

Just before touching the tape Bikila lifted his hands slightly. Officials immediately rushed towards him but he made to touch his toes and jog a little on the spot. Niskanen burst through the line to embrace his pupil. What now shocked observers was how calm Bikila seemed in the aftermath of victory. He was brought a blanket, wrote Lechenperg, "but he waves it away." Then: "His face is transfigured; he looks around as if to make sure where he is. Then the tension begins to subside and he laughs. Only after a while does he calm down, and his laughter gives way to tears that stream down his cheeks."

His time was a record 2 hours 15 minutes 16.2 seconds. This was eight minutes faster than Emil Zatopek's 1952 Olympic triumph. Within minutes Bikila was hoisted aloft and laughing for joy.

Twenty-six seconds after Bikila had crossed the line Rhadi came in too. Bikila slapped him on the back to congratulate him. Later Rhadi gave an explanation as to why it was not him who had won the gold. Although cited in Lunzenfichter's account, some have expressed doubts about it. Lunzenfichter, however, would certainly not have quoted this if he did not believe it to be true. "I lost my chance stupidly," he said. Towards the end he said he had seen some taut ropes, "just as at the end of a cross-country race."

> I thought the race was finished. After having passed between the ropes I stopped but Bikila continued. The end was a few hundred metres further on. A Frenchman in the crowd came towards me shouting that I had to go on because the race was not yet finished ... I started again but Abebe Bikila had already won the race.

After the race Niskanen asked Bikila what it had felt like when Rhadi had started to lag. He replied:

> The rattling sound of footsteps on the cobble-stones faded away when I increased the pace right inside the town walls. When I increased it a little bit more there was no sound at all. I didn't need to turn around to check because if you had heard these steps for the last hour you knew what it meant when they faded away. And I was happy, not because I was afraid of a sprinting battle, but it was nice to get rid of that stubborn Moroccan.

Almost immediately after he had won, Bikila was examined by a doctor. He had only one word to say: "Fantastico!" Bikila's pulse rate stood at a mere 88, his eyes were clear, he showed no signs of fatigue and there were no indications of bruising on his bare feet. He then told Niskanen that he could have kept going for another 10 to 15 kilometres at the same speed!

Wearing his tracksuit Bikila now proudly accepted the gold medal and waved to the crowds. Rhadi stood beside him with Barry Magee who had won the bronze. Behind them were the floodlit Arch of Constantine and the flagpoles. After being presented with the medals the three flags were run up, the Ethiopian being, of course, the highest one and in the centre.

Robert Parienté of the French sports newspaper, *L'Equipe*, had been invited by the organising committee to follow the marathon in the helicopter from where some of the film's sequences were shot. This is his account: "I saw Rhadi go ahead and then I saw a black man who was running barefoot. We did not know who he was. Then we looked at the lists and did not know if his surname was Abebe or Bikila." Kihachiro Onitsuka, the head of a then small Japanese sports shoe company bearing his name, which would later become the giant Asics corporation, remembers Bikila's victory in similar terms. Because of the nature of his business Onitsuka says that it was a reflex action of his to look first at an athlete's feet and only then at his face: "You can imagine my surprise when I saw the bare feet of this runner who was breaking a world record then his black face which, to my neighbours and myself, was totally unknown! Everybody was asking: 'What number is he? What number is he?'"

What had just happened, explains Parienté, was simply stunning. In athletics, he says, there are no "spontaneous generations". That is to say that athletes work their way up the scales and through the competitions and so, by the time they reach the top, they are generally well known. So, he says, sporting generations "develop". And it was this that made Bikila extraordinary: "He was the spontaneous generation. We had never ever heard of him, he'd never been out of his own country."[1] For Parienté, the second "amazing thing" about Bikila and Rome was that he, and it, marked "the emergence of Africa."

Bikila's triumph was celebrated not just in Ethiopia but across the continent. He was the first black African to win a gold medal at the Olympics. For a moment his triumph captured the new spirit of Africa, the zeitgeist, the "winds of change" sweeping the continent. With Ghana's independence in 1957, the whole of black Africa

1. *This we now know to be untrue, as he had been to Sweden with Niskanen in 1958.*

stood at the brink of independence and a glorious new future. And Bikila was its symbol. Poor, yes, barefoot yes – but victorious. Bikila had struck a blow not just for Ethiopia but for a generation of Africans for whom the future still seemed so bright, despite the ominous chaos which was at the very same moment rocking the newly independent former Belgian Congo. How much of this Bikila understood is questionable but one man who did comprehend the significance of his triumph was Yidnekatchew Tessema. He had been listening to the race commentary on the radio. As it wore on and it became clear that Bikila was now up in front:

> We were immersed in a deep feeling of ecstasy and awe as we heard that report … Soon Abebe appeared flanked by two burning torches on his left and right side and we picked up our jackets and put them on proudly to show our country designation (Ethiopia) and jumped into the field to meet our hero as he ran through the finishing ribbon. We rushed on him and embraced him with an excitement never experienced before. It was at this point that Abebe whispered into my ear the unforgettable words "Haven't I fulfilled your wish?" Soon Ethiopia's victory inspired a holiday mood, one can say, among the entire residents of Rome, and our corner of the Olympic village, which had hardly attracted any attention in the past few days, was surrounded by journalists and television cameramen. Abebe Wakjira finished seventh in the event that day. Since it was my 39th birthday, I celebrated both occasions together. That event was not only Ethiopia's victory. It was also a historic day for Africa because it was the first time an African country had won a gold medal in the Olympics. My happiness that day rose to such a height that I saw Abebe's victory as marking the beginning of a new chapter in the history of sports

in Ethiopia.

Today, it is taken for granted that Africans are good at sports; then they were an almost unknown quantity. Black sportsmen had been champions before but, like Jesse Owens in the 1936 Berlin Olympics, they had been mostly black Americans. White South Africans and Arab North Africans had also long been well represented in the Olympic medals stakes. Although black African participation, especially in early games, was rare, it was not unknown. In the third modern Olympics, held in 1904 in Saint Louis, two black South Africans, Tswanas called Len Tau and Jan Mashiani came 9th and 12th respectively in the marathon. They were the first black Africans to compete in the games and did so in rather haphazard circumstances, since they were actually in St Louis to participate in shows at the concurrent World Fair, in which hundreds of South Africans had come to stage re-enactments of Boer War battles. So, Bikila's victory was the beginning of something new. To understand the impact Bikila made it is important to bear this in mind.

From a specifically Ethiopian point of view Colonel Bekele Gezaw notes that Bikila's victory was particularly sweet, especially for the older generation. This was because the marathon had passed through the Piazza Venezia, and then ended only a stone's throw away from it. It was from here, from the balcony of the Palazzo Venezia that Mussolini had announced the beginning of his Ethiopian campaign 25 years before. It was doubly pleasurable then that the victor should be a member of Haile Selassie's own personal guard.

Curiously, this point of view was not one that was

shared by all Ethiopians. Fekrou Kidane was later to become a senior official of the International Olympic Committee in Lausanne. Before that he was, for many years, Yidnekatchew Tessema's right hand man as secretary-general of the Ethiopian Olympic Committee. He says that the symbolism of the obelisk of Axum was lost on the vast majority of Ethiopians since only a handful of intellectuals had ever heard of it. As for the victory in Rome itself he claims that it was western journalists who spun the line of Ethiopia's revenge: "Ethiopians didn't relate to this. The Italians are very nice people and after the war many of them stayed in Ethiopia. There was no antagonism and no feeling of revenge." Besides he notes, until then at least, Ethiopians like other Africans were more interested in football than anything else in sport.

Interestingly, there is an echo of Kidane's viewpoint in the memory of many Italians too. They were over-joyed that a barefoot Ethiopian should become one of the champions of their games too. Primo Nebiolo, one of the father figures of the Italian sports world, who then became the controversial and powerful head of the IAAF until his death in 1999, recalled:

> We were happy. Despite the history of the war we had had long links with Ethiopia and it was a country we loved. In fact whenever someone from Ethiopia or [the former Italian colonies of] Somalia, Eritrea or Libya wins it delights us because we feel close to them … we feel there's something of us there.

Nebiolo, who was present when Bikila won, also remembered that no one knew who he was. "Africans were not so strong in sport at that time. It was a great surprise and we were happy about it. He was a nice boy, sweet, very kind – and one of the greatest athletes we have ever had."

Mention the name Bikila today and prompt with the words "barefoot marathon runner," and it is amazing how many people have, at the very least, some recollection of him. In Italy, however, his name remains totally fresh. It is truly extraordinary how many people there can either remember him or know who he was – and even know what became of him. For people in their fifties there is also another phenomenon at work here. They remember Bikila as the champion of Rome but also say that he was the first African they had ever really heard of.

For Ottavio Castellini, a marathon historian and statistician, the experience of watching Bikila's victory live on television at the age of 15 sparked a lifelong interest in the marathon. He says that until Bikila and Mamo Wolde brought the attention of the sport to the public eye it had been very much the poor relation of the track and field athletics family. Since 1960, Castellini has followed the sport more assiduously than almost anyone else and for him Bikila's victory in Rome was an incredibly emotional moment. There was, he explains, the "mystery" of the unknown barefoot black runner coupled with the majesty of ancient Rome by night. Although Bikila was to go on to win in Tokyo in 1964 and to become a sporting phenomenon celebrated far and wide, the magic of Rome was never to be repeated.

Today, Bikila still lives in the memory of Romans but it would be unfair and inaccurate to say that he is remembered as the sole champion of the games. He is one of a triumvirate. The other two were Livio Berutti, the Italian sprinter and 200 metre record breaker, and the American, Wilma Rudolph.

Dubbed the "black gazelle", Wilma Rudolph was a beautiful 20-year-old black American, whom it seems every male present fell in love with. She took three gold medals, winning the 100 metres, the 200 metres and the 4 x 100 metres. Her story, a curious mirror image of Bikila's, was one of tragedy *into* triumph. From the age of four to eleven she had been paralysed with polio.

For Giacomo Mazzocchi the games, and particularly Bikila's win, were a "fantastic fantasy of incredible sensation. For us Berutti represented Europe and Wilma Rudolph the symbol of the American desire to succeed." However, he adds: "We always support the poor and the underdog and so Bikila entered our hearts this way. He became a hero."

5. Homecomings

The events of the next two months were as dramatic as those two hours in Rome. Bikila returned home a conquering hero – before barely escaping with his life as Ethiopia began its long and tortuous descent into chaos, war and terror.

Before arriving home, the plane carrying the Olympians stopped in Khartoum. This was the site of a minor incident of which Bikila would probably not have understood the undertones, or at least not then. Following his victory, the commanders of the Imperial Bodyguard had sent a regimental uniform up to Khartoum. The idea was that it would be taken on board so that Bikila could change into it and emerge from the plane, once it touched down in Addis Ababa, dressed in full uniform. Exactly who was involved in the quarrel over the uniform is unclear but eventually it was decided that Bikila would not wear it but rather leave the plane wearing the suit he had been issued with, which was embroidered with the Ethiopian symbol. According to Colonel Bekele Gezaw, he did not wear the uniform because "it would have been a symbol of the Guard and not of Ethiopia". The significance of this was only to become apparent several weeks later.

From early morning, thousands began to gather at the airport to welcome Bikila. On the tarmac the bands of the Imperial Bodyguard, the Police and the Army also took up position. As the plane began its descent the crowd broke into wild cheering.

Many people had come at the urging of the media. While it was clear to Ethiopia's educated people that Bikila had scored a great patriotic victory, this was not at first evident to many others. Apart from the fact that most Ethiopians, if they were interested in sports, were mainly football fans, many simply could not understand what the fuss was all about. After all everyone in the countryside ran long distances every day as they herded their cattle. Only when it was explained that Bikila had struck a blow for Ethiopia by running faster than the fastest white man did the full significance of his victory dawn on the whole country.

As the plane touched down part of the crowd surged forward. According to Tsige Abebe, one journalist managed to get on board the plane before Bikila could get out. If she is to be believed, he provided the following wooden answers to the following wooden questions:

"Everybody gets fatigued when running, and I am sure you must have been tired at some point in the course of the race. What provided you with solace and endurance at those moments?" Abebe replied, "It was the responsibility given to me as a member of the Imperial Bodyguard that served as the source of my comfort as well as endurance." Next the reporter urged Abebe to look outside the window where he was seated, and then asked him, "Did you ever, at any point in your trip, imagine that a huge crowd would gather to welcome you home?" Abebe's response was,

"Although I never expected this much I guessed that the people of Ethiopia would await me with joy."

Wearing his gold medal Bikila now emerged from the plane. A special spot was reserved for him on the tarmac. Here he was garlanded with wreaths, from the Mayor of Addis Ababa, from the President of the Sports Federation and, of course, Brigadier-General Mengistu Neway, the Commander of the Imperial Bodyguard. Others who had come to the airport included the Chief of Staff of the Ethiopian Army, top sports officials and the American ambassador. Wudinesh, Bikila's mother and Yewebdar, his wife, were also there. They kissed him on both cheeks and gave him their own flowers. Bikila made a speech of thanks before beginning his triumphal procession into the city. Tsige Abebe notes:

> Before he entered the special open vehicle readied to transport him to the heart of the city, he took a moment to once again take a look at Yewebdar and his mother who once disapproved of his running routine. What he read in her eyes, given their first exposure to such a spectacle, was bewilderment.

Tens of thousands lined the route, cheering Bikila and singing a specially composed song. Everyone who was there still remembers the scene. At the front of the procession a platform had been fixed over the engine of an army jeep on which was chained a two-year-old lion. This was Makuria, who was not just the symbol of Ethiopia but also the Imperial Guard, regarded as its living emblem.

Bikila waved to the crowds from the top of the converted lorry on which had been built a small platform. On two sides of it was an iron grille fashioned in the shape of the Olympic rings. People tossed confetti and rose petals before the champion. So many crowded the route that at times the procession could only inch forward. Some walked alongside playing shepherd's flutes.

At the palace, Bikila was presented to the Emperor and Empress in the Green Salon. Haile Selassie then decorated Bikila with the Star of Ethiopia. There is a picture of the two face to face. Bikila, his star hanging from his jacket, looks tense in the presence of Selassie. The Emperor, shorter by half a head, looks straight ahead, tired, even somewhat distracted.

Abebe Wakjira recalls that the Emperor said: "Thanks to both of you. In the name of all Ethiopians you have won a great victory." Wakjira was then handed an envelope containing 150 Birr, then $75. He recalls: "Bikila got one too but I don't know how much was in his." Bikila was also promoted to the rank of corporal. Tsige Abebe records that the Emperor then made the following speech:

> We are definitely pleased to see today the first fruit of the sports organisation that We started in Our reign. Finding ourselves international victors in such a sport as would demand physical fitness and endurance makes Ethiopia even more worthy of International Recognition. With your achievement serving as a trailblazer, the door has now been opened for future generations to follow in your footsteps.

The last sentence at least was to prove truer than the Emperor could possibly have imagined. After the palace, according to the *Voice of Ethiopia* newspaper: "Again escorted by a long line of cars and receiving cheers from thousands lined along the route, the Olympic hero drove to his new residence. Later a luncheon party was tendered in his honour by the Imperial Guard."

There were more than a thousand people at the party. They included all the commanders of the Imperial Bodyguard, who were paying for the feast. Bikila was now given use of a chauffeur-driven white Volkswagen Beetle, which belonged to the Guard. It had to be chauffeur-driven, as Bikila did not yet know how to drive. He was in great demand and needed the transport to pay visits around the country. Bikila was also moved into a Guard-owned house, which is the residence that the newspaper refers to and was a significant improvement on his previous, modest home.

Phil Pilley wrote later in *World Sports* that: "Rumours of gifts in cash and kind, even of a rent free home, caused true-blue eyebrows to raise in the sophisticated strongholds of western amateurism." It is important to remember that this was a time when sportsmen were not supposed to make money from being sportsmen but rather to compete for the love of sport alone.

The next few weeks were ones of hectic parties and receptions. After one, just after he returned, the *Ethiopian Herald* newspaper wrote that Bikila was "escorted to his residence which was fantastically decorated with flags and flowers and crowded with admirers and fans. A luncheon ... was held. To highlight the occasion the Imperial Body Guard Theatrical Group sang and danced to the delight of Abebe, the Olympians, relatives and others present."

Bikila and Niskanen. (Niskanen collection)

Niskanen and Bikila, who has signed the picture. (Niskanen collection)

Father Christmas Niskanen (plus one ...) at one of Emperor Haile Selassie's
Christmas parties. (Niskanen collection)

Swedish Embassy party. Niskanen is in the dark, dress uniform.
(Niskanen collection)

Niskanen was a founder of the Ethiopian Highland Rally. (Niskanen collection)

Niskanen and friend. (Niskanen collection)

In training. Wami Biratu is wearing white, on the far left. Mamo Wolde and Bikila (right) lead the pack. (Niskanen collection)

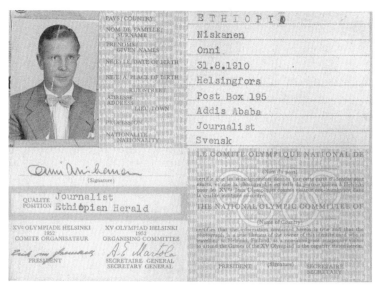

Niskanen, journalist of the *Ethiopian Herald*. Helsinki Olympics, 1952. (Niskanen collection)

Bikila in training. Note the other man, running to work perhaps?
(Niskanen collection)

Wami Biratu, Bikila and Niskanen. Tokyo 1964. (Niskanen collection)

Bikila, Tokyo marathon, 1964. (Getty Images)

Bikila wins gold in Tokyo. On his right, Basil Heatley of Britain who won silver, on his left, Kokichi Tsuburaya of Japan who won the bronze. October 1964. (Getty Images)

Mexico, 20 October 1968. Bikila, in pain, in the middle.
(Niskanen collection)

Niskanen and his new champion, Mamo Wolde. (Niskanen collection)

Bikila and Niskanen, probably at Bikila's
home in Addis Ababa.
(Niskanen collection)

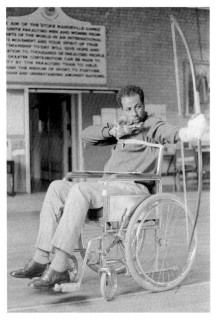

Bikila practises archery from his wheel-
chair in preparation for the International
Paraplegic Games, 20 July 1970.
(Getty Images)

The front page of the paper of the same day, September 17th, also contained an announcement of a "buffet-dancing party" to be held by the Ethiopian Patriotic Association Club that evening. There Bikila was presented with a gold watch and, on behalf of a sports association he was given "a big wall clock". Abebe Wakjira was given a "table clock". Almost forty years later Wakjira, in his home in the little town of Fiche, still had his, although it no longer worked.

Pilley wrote that on November 2nd, which was the 30th anniversary of Haile Selassie's coronation, "life for the soldier-athlete was hectically happy." And Bikila had more to celebrate than his Olympic victory alone. Yewebdar, who had been pregnant during the games, now gave birth to their first child, a son named Geremo. What may not have been immediately clear though was that Geremo was a sickly baby and possibly handicapped. Later Bikila's friend, Hailu Abebe, recalled that this was to make him "very sad" and that he did all he could to care for his son, taking him "to be blessed in holy waters at different places across the country and to the Imperial Bodyguard hospital."

Meanwhile, as Bikila celebrated and General Mengistu Neway toasted his guardsman champion, it is now clear that the commander of the Guards had other things on his mind. Along with his brother Girmame, and a few others, he was plotting a coup and the overthrow of the Emperor. Ryszard Kapuscinski, the famous Polish journalist, described General Mengistu, in his classic book on the fall of Haile Selassie, *The Emperor*, as an: "officer of fearless character and uncommon masculine good looks." Girmame, believed to be the brains behind the coup, was something of an intellectual. He had studied in the United States, gaining a master's degree from Columbia. On his return he had become a civil servant who, according to Hans Wilhelm Lockot – a German who worked in Ethiopia at the time and wrote *The Mission*, an important biography of Haile Selassie – was a man with a "high sense of civic responsibility and concern for the underprivileged" that made him "suspect in the eyes of the regime" which exiled him to distant administrative posts. Michael Lentakis, the Ethiopian born Greek who says that Niskanen originally noticed Bikila running everyday from Sululta, is less circumspect. Girmame he claims was "a fanatic communist who did not hide his hatred for everything European." Other plotters included the Head of the Imperial Police, the chief of palace security and other members of the Emperor's inner circle. It is impossible to imagine a plot involving more trusted or senior people - bar the leadership of the Army itself.

The coup was scheduled to begin during the night of 13th -14th December, a day after Haile Selassie had arrived in Brazil for a state visit. Just before he left, Haile Selassie said to General Mengistu: "I leave the country in your hands."

Wami Biratu recalls that when he first heard about the coup, on the morning of the 14th December, he was playing hockey. Soldiers and officers were suddenly ordered to arm, but they had no clear idea what was going on. Biratu noted that many officers were at home and so was Bikila. He thinks that it is possible that Bikila had had a tip-off and decided to stay away from the Guard's headquarters that day. Others dismiss this in the strongest possible terms. They say that Bikila was utterly insignificant in this affair and that it is inconceivable that he would have been informed of what was coming.

Members of the Imperial family and other loyalists were now confined to the palace while Asfa Wossen, the Emperor's son, with whom relations had been cool, read out a proclamation on the radio. Later he was to say that he had been forced to do this at gunpoint, a claim that is widely accepted in Ethiopia. The proclamation read:

> The people of Ethiopia have waited for the day when poverty and backwardness would cease to be, but nothing has been achieved after innumerable promises. No other nation has borne so much in patience.

Lentakis recalls hearing the speech. Shops had begun to close, government employees were going home and soldiers were on the streets. He decided to go to a bar called the Trianon where large numbers of Greeks and Ethiopians were listening to "the trembling voice" of Asfa Wossen whose proclamation was being repeated every ten minutes. As if all this was not bad enough, what struck particular terror into the hearts of many foreigners was that the statement also said that the country was exploited not just by the feudal aristocratic class, but also by the Greeks, the Armenians and the Arabs, "and that this had to stop." Then the radio played a song called *Rise Up* and another song, which had been a hit of the band of the Imperial Bodyguard called *I Cannot*. Lentakis notes that it was originally a popular love song, but "the words had a double meaning, saying that patience was exhausted and that a change was needed."

Alerted via the Ethiopian Embassy in London, Haile Selassie began the long trek home. By the time the plane had reached Chad one of its engines had broken down. But the Emperor said that he had no intention of waiting for it to be repaired and so the plane took off again for Khartoum where another aircraft would be waiting. "Whose life is it you are trembling for, yours or mine?" he demanded of the crew and his entourage. When he finally touched down in Asmara in Eritrea he was greeted with the usual pomp and ceremony. A crisis meeting was now held with governors and ministers. The Emperor was shocked when he realised just how many of the people he had trusted were in revolt against him.

At the beginning of the coup some life had continued as normal in Addis Ababa. This was partly because, despite the proclamation, few people knew what was happening. Radios were still a luxury. The coup was to fail however, because the Guard had not secured the support of the Army and they were badly organised. On the third day, regiments loyal to the Emperor (who was not yet back, entered the suburbs. General Mengistu went to the university to meet the students. Ryszard Kapuscinski writes:

> He shows them a piece of dry bread. "This," he says, "is what we fed to the dignitaries today, so that they will know what our people live on. You must help us." Shooting breaks out in the city. The battle for Addis Ababa begins. Hundreds meet their death in the streets.

The leader of the Army who was now mobilising his forces to crush the rebels was none other than Lieutenant General Merid Mengesha, who had used his influence with the Emperor to make sure that Niskanen was included on the trip to Rome.

The fighting came right into the heart of the city, with shells exploding inside the palace. Just as the Guards rebellion collapsed, though, many of those closest to the Emperor (the exact number is unclear) were massacred inside the palace, in the Green Salon where Bikila had been greeted by the Emperor on his return. Since the Army and Imperial Bodyguard had the same uniform, many were killed by their own side and there were gruesome scenes in the city. "Hundreds of bodies were laying around, unburied and rotting," recalls Lentakis, "and thousands of vultures were having a field day." Hundreds of hyenas had also come down, from the Entoto Hills he says, to start "their macabre dinner." Then, the Guards tried to withdraw in the direction of the hills, where Niskanen had been regularly training his protégé. A bloodbath ensued.

As gunfire died down the Emperor returned. It was to be the second great homecoming in just over two months – but an altogether very different one to Bikila's. At the airport Haile Selassie was met by the Patriarch, the army commander and ministers. Hans Wilhelm Lockot records the following in his book *The Mission*:

> The Crown Prince was there too, carrying a stone on his shoulder – the traditional sign of submission in Ethiopia – and prostrating himself before his father. Haile Selassie ordered him to stand, and dismissed the gesture of the stone. The Crown Prince, he was told,

had acted under duress, with a gun in his ribs. But nobody could manipulate Haile Selassie. According to a popular version, he replied: "And you didn't know that your last hour had come? You have not learned to die like an Emperor."

The Emperor then proceeded to return to his palace. The scene was dramatic. As Lockot recalls, the city had just before been filled with the sounds of mourning.

> As the evening advanced, there came a sudden silence, and then from the direction of the airport, far away, a peculiar sound could be heard, faint at first, but resolving itself, as it became louder, into a mass of human voices. As it came nearer, the wave of sound rolled over the town. Everywhere, on all sides, came cries and shouts from the huts and the houses. The men's voices united in a hollow roar, interspersed by women's high-pitched yodelling, the traditional Ethiopian sound of jubilation. People came out of their homes, the masters of wealthier households along with their servants. While those lining the route from the airport cheered the Emperor as he passed, he himself sat in the open car stony-faced. Some actually prostrated themselves on the ground, praying and thanking God as the motorcade, with its escort of armoured vehicles, sped past.

General Mengistu and his brother escaped but were eventually surrounded by peasants hoping for a reward. According to one of several differing accounts Mengistu shot his brother dead before trying to kill himself. He failed – but wounded himself in the eye. He was then put on trial and finally hung at dawn on 13 March 1961 in the main square of Addis Ababa. The pressure of the noose made his eyeball pop out.

And what of Bikila during this turbulent period? What follows is the official version of what happened to him. It was published in the *Ethiopian Herald* on 23 December 1960 and there appears to be no reason to disbelieve it. There is no evidence that Bikila ever had a political thought in his life.

MARATHON STAR ABEBE SAFE & SOUND

Corporal Abebe Bikilla [sic], the Ethiopian Marathon winner and member of the Imperial Body Guard called at the Ethiopian Sports Federation headquarters yesterday having safely escaped those critical days of last week.

The Marathon champion looked fine and strong with a few additional pounds.

Rumours spread earlier that Abebe had been injured. Foreign radio stations were also speculating on his whereabouts; some assumed that Abebe Bikilla had died or been seriously injured during the clashes, being a member of the Imperial Body Guard.

Interviewed yesterday at the office of the Secretary General of the Ethiopian Football Federation, Ato Yednekatchew Tessema, Corporal Abebe said that he had not taken part in the fighting during the rebellion.[1] On the morning of the abortive coup d'etat, the runner stated, he was told at his headquarters that there was no need to report for duty. He then returned to his house and remained there with his family throughout the fighting.

He said he had not understood the nature and cause of the plot "until late on Friday, the third day."

"I reported to the First Police Station last Saturday» Abebe declared, "and said that I just belonged to the sports section of the Body Guard and never took part in the action."

---

1. *This is the same Yidnekatchew who had been to Rome with Bikila less than two months before.*

He then obtained a pass from the Police Chief and was walking home when he was caught by the loyalist army forces and was led to the former 3rd Regiment headquarter (at Jan Hoy Meda), for detention. However he was immediately released by Colonel Jagama Kello, having obtained another free pass from him.

He now reports twice daily at this headquarter.

Hailu Abebe, a friend of Bikila, a 10,000 metre runner and another Guard confirms the gist of the story, including that of Bikila's own brief detention. He says: "It was a big shock. We were very surprised and had no idea what was happening."

Wami Biratu was in charge of 38 men during the coup. He says that he had been ordered to take up positions and to fight the Army when they came. According to him, he and his men did not fight because the Army never approached them. However, as with almost all the other Guards, he was subsequently detained. There then followed an incident for which Biratu has clearly still not forgiven Bikila. The champion appeared at the detention camp and used his influence to have his friend Tilahun Gessese released. Gessese, who was also a Guardsman, was also a famous singer. Bikila did nothing to help Biratu. "Of course I was angry," he says.

Later Biratu's father was told that his son was dead and he came to see Bikila to ask for his help. Bikila said he knew nothing and clearly did nothing. Biratu remained in detention for 28 days.

After the coup, most of the surviving Guards were disbanded and dispersed but according to Biratu "the sportsmen were told to stay". As for Bikila, it was now clearer than ever that he was far too precious a prize to lose. One newspaper remarked baldly: "Abebe owes his life to gold medal". Tadele Yidnekatchew, the son of Yidnekatchew Tessema, an urbane and sophisticated man who now runs a building company in Addis Aba-ba, confirms the story about Bikila knowing nothing of the tumultuous events and says that his father moved to "protect" Bikila "in case he said anything stupid."

Tsige Abebe's account varies little from the others except that she does not say he was released immediately. She says that her father was training for Christmas sports competitions at the *Jan Hoy* field when the coup began and that he spent 24 hours in detention.

Whether Niskanen had any contact with Bikila during these nervous days is unknown. However, we do know that working with only one assistant, he saved many lives by organising an ambulance to pick up the injured. Curt Erik Dahlborn, a cheerful Swede who was then working with the police, recalls that Niskanen, carrying his Red Cross boxes, criss-crossed the whole town by foot, the only European to do so, "helping people he saw bleeding.[2] There is also a report that, because he knew people on both sides, Niskanen, with the American ambassador, attempted to mediate but that their efforts came to naught. Certainly, that is the case with the latter and perhaps Niskanen tried to help him.

In retrospect, we can see that the events of that week were to mark the beginning of the end for Haile Selassie and the now ossifying ancien regime. However, the end was to take another fourteen years in coming. This

---

2. *In 1987, Niskanen was posthumously awarded the Henry Dunant medal by the Red Cross, the highest honour it can bestow. He was also honoured by the Ethiopian Red Cross. The citation for the former said it was for his work in Ethiopia and internationally and called him an "outstanding example of humanity."*

period coincided almost exactly with the rest of Bikila's life, which at its end, was marked by tragedy too. In the meantime, as the reputation of Haile Selassie began to crumbleand - should read to crumble and most westerners remembered him only for his stand against Mussolini; Bikila was a valuable asset. His prowess could be used to prop up the image of the regime as, it began its slow descent into chaos. The historian Bahru Zewde wrote later that:

> The torch of change that the rebels had kindled was not extinguished with their physical elimination. On the contrary, it sparked a more outspoken and radical opposition to the regime. This can be seen in some of the underground leaflets that began to circulate soon after the end of the coup. They had such uncompromising motifs as "Better be a lion for a day and die than live the life of a lamb for a thousand days", "There is no solution without blood", and "What is sinful is to be ruled by despots, not to rise against them." Above all, the students became the true heirs of the rebels. They had come out on the streets in support of the rebels in 1960. Thereafter, they gave breadth and coherence to the opposition that the rebels had conceived and executed in such a confused manner. As for the regime, unprepared to concede reform, it condemned itself to being swept away by revolution.

6. A Champion's Life

The coup began on a Wednesday and was finished on Sunday. By all accounts Monday was a normal day.

After Rome though, no day would ever be normal for Bikila again. Although still a Guardsman he had few, if any, regular duties to perform. He was now, more than ever, a sports machine. He played tennis, football, hockey and basketball and when he was not playing he was watching. He liked to enjoy himself; he went dancing and played billiards. He was also now on the international sports circuit and in this period his eyes remained firmly focused on the new goal; the Tokyo Olympics of 1964.

After his victory in 1960, Bikila gave a typically terse interview to the *Ethiopian Herald*. It bears mention here. Asked whether he thought he could repeat his triumph four years later he said: "Fighters never think of losing … they always go out on the assumption that the victory is always theirs." Asked about his health the reporter noted: "Having stolen a glance at the predominantly fat audience, the soldier animated [sic]: 'if you keep yourself in good shape, you can never be too old for the Olympics even at 40.'"

Bikila's record in these years, however, was mixed.

Although he was winning more often than not, his timings nowhere near matched his Olympic record. He had some poor performances in Scandinavia and came second to Mamo Wolde in San Sebastian. His wins came in Athens, Osaka and Kosice in Slovakia.

The Greek run was staged on 7 May 1961 and was to begin in the legendary village of Marathon itself. It was only his second international marathon. Before the race started there were some festivities, which included traditional dancing, and even some religious ceremonies. As a warm up the athletes participated in the dancing, which went on until the race started. In September 1961, Niskanen wrote an account of what happened for the *Svenskbladet*, the Swedish community newspaper in Ethiopia. He reminded his readers that because of the hills the course is "probably one of the toughest that exists":

> Abebe took the lead immediately after the start. After a couple of minutes he was alone and didn't see another runner for the rest of the race. I was in one of the lead cars but due to the narrow roads I didn't catch up with him until the 9th kilometre mark. He was then already almost a kilometre in front of the other runners and I told him to slow down a little. The first ten kilometres were done in 29 mins 44 sec which says it all. We have no runner in Sweden who does 10 kilometres at that speed.

The last ten kilometres were farcical. The course was lined with people who kept tossing flowers at Abebe. He felt it rude to throw them away, so he would run with them until he could pass them on to some beautiful girl further down the road. Then he would get another bouquet. "As luck would have it," wrote Niskanen, "he had a good lead and could afford to take the time."

Bikila's time was 2 hours 23 minutes 44 seconds. Second was the Belgian Aurele Vandendriessche who was to take his revenge in Boston a few months later. At the awards ceremony in the old Athens Olympic stadium Bikila received an olive leaf wreath and the winner's trophy handed to him by the Ethiopian ambassador. A little girl from the embassy also gave Bikila a bouquet of flowers "almost as big as herself." Niskanen also writes, almost as an aside, that while everyone had been waiting for the marathon runners to come in, the spectators had been watching some other "general" athletics. "Gosta Olander from Valadalen ran around filming it all. He gave Abebe Bikila and myself a standing invitation to his house in Valadalen if we should have the chance to visit Sweden." Olander was, of course, the great Swedish trainer who had been Niskanen's inspiration. It is a pity that we do not know what passed between the three men since Bikila, thanks to Niskanen, was the final product, the vindication of Olander's ideas. For the Swedes at least, the moment must have been rather emotional.

On 15 June 1961, Bikila, Biratu and Niskanen went to Japan to participate in the Mainichi marathon in Osaka. Mainichi are one of Japan's major media groups. It was the first time Wami Biratu had ever been abroad. The trip was to mark another important first though: Niskanen decided that Bikila had to wear shoes. The race was to be held on June 25th so there was time to train. Several kilometres of the course were on gravel and, writes Niskanen, "in other places there was poor tarmac. In Rome and Athens [Abebe] had run barefoot, but this time I didn't dare take the risk of bruised feet. Wami had to run barefoot as he had never run with shoes on."

Kihachiro Onitsuka, the head of the sports shoe company, who had witnessed Bikila's victory in Rome, managed to secure an introduction via his friend, the Mainichi sports reporter Kohei Murakuso, a former athlete who had run the 10,000 and 5,000 metres at the 1936 Berlin Olympics. Onitsuka was clearly the right man in the right place at the right time. "I was very impressed," he remarked. "I had the feeling I was dealing with a philosopher rather than a runner." Thirty-six years later, this is how he recalled the meeting.

> *Onitsuka*: I am here to support you and supply you with shoes. I hope you will win this race with my shoes!
> *Bikila*: I have always run barefoot and I have won many times. I don't need shoes.
> *Onitsuka*: The roads in Japan are very rough and that's why you should wear shoes.
> *Bikila*: The roads may be rough but I don't need shoes.
> *Onitsuka*: Your bare feet are excellent, they are like cat's paws. But still, shoes could improve your records.

At this point Niskanen intervened and persuaded Bikila that Onitsuka might be right. Bikila bowed to his judgement. There is a photo, which shows Onitsuka and Bikila together. The Japanese, who is wearing a bow tie, is crouched down trying a hand tailored white "Tiger" training shoe on Bikila's foot. The runner, who is sitting on a bed, is wearing white shorts and white socks. On the bed next to him is a black shoe, one of the type he would in the end wear for the marathon.

The Ethiopians took the lead of the 51 runners immediately despite the heat and the 87% humidity. "The climate was dreadful," Niskanen wrote later, "I have never in my life seen runners sweat as much as that day. Abebe didn't have a dry spot on his shirt or his trousers." Normally Niskanen would not give his runners anything to drink before 35 kilometres but here he had to give them refreshments, fruit juice with glucose, every five kilometres after the 20 kilometre mark. Biratu got salt tablets too, which help prevent cramps and other ailments during marathons, but he now developed a stomach upset and could not keep up with Bikila.

As he was so far in the lead Niskanen wrote that he "ran alone" but he then corrected himself: "Alone is perhaps the wrong word. Perhaps a million people lined the road of the race. I have never seen a more enthusiastic public." The race was also Bikila's first encounter with live television broadcasts and, according to his account, Niskanen fought a running battle to make sure Bikila had a clear run:

> Abebe was continuously surrounded by cars filled with TV cameras, photographers, journalists and administrators. From time to time groups of motorbikes squeezed through and almost drowned poor Abebe in their fumes. No one thought of the damage they were doing. I tried on several occasions to point out to the administrators in my car that they should remove some of the cars and motorbikes, so that Abebe could run in peace without, from time to time, having to shy away from nosy photographers. It helped for a few minutes, but was soon just as bad again. No one did it

out of ill will, that was clear. Everyone wished to film and photograph as closely as possible.

Despite the problem, the run turned into, as Niskanen notes quoting the papers, a "one man show". Bikila won with a time of 2 hours 29 minutes 27 seconds. He came in ten minutes quicker than Biratu who, Niskanen records, "not only had to fight the heat, but also his stomach upset and bruised feet in the last 12 kilometres." Biratu came second, the third place going to a runner who came in 17 seconds after him.

After the race, Bikila told Onitsuka, the shoemaker: "You were right, they gave me more grip and better tracking." Onitsuka, whose company was renamed Asics in 1977, and which was to become a huge and successful corporation recalls that that moment was one of the best of his career. He died, aged 89, in 2007.

At the end of his article for *Svenksbladet* in which he had written up the experiences of Rome, Athens and Osaka, Niskanen added the following:

> Abebe Bikila's success has in every respect opened the possibilities for athletics in Ethiopia. Interest has grown and especially for long distance running. It is no longer difficult to get the boys to train. Those who are interested in seeing how Abebe runs can go and see the Olympic film, now showing at the Haile Selassie 1 Theatre. It's worth it!

In October, in Kosice, Bikila won again, with a time of 2 hours 20 minutes 12 seconds.

In 1962, Bikila competed in several, generally shorter events. These included races in Berlin, Malmo and Copenhagen. While they were in Sweden, Niskanen, Bikila and Mamo Wolde went to stay with Magnus Ehrenstrom who had invited them for a rest at his home in Strangnas, a small, lakeside town dating back to Viking times, about 90 kilometres west of Stockholm. He had been one of the serving Swedish officers in Ethiopia and in 1966 was to become general-secretary of *Radda Barnen*, Swedish Save the Children. While he had been in Ethiopia he had shared the Rubin's sauna with both the athletes and with Niskanen. His observation is that, because they came from simple backgrounds, they were "shy" and "modest" in the presence of foreigners, but always "very polite."

In 1963, Bikila flew to the US to take part in the Boston marathon with Mamo Wolde. Its importance lay in the fact that it was the last world class marathon before Tokyo. As there is no record of Niskanen having been there we may assume that this was one of the first, if not the first foreign trip that they had taken without him. Bikila stayed with the family of one Dr Warren Guild in Lexington, just outside Boston, where the American revolution had begun in 1775. Later, Guild recalled that Bikila had "more dedication and courage per square pound of human flesh than anyone I have ever known."

For Bikila, Boston was not a success even though he was the favourite. In an interview with a Boston paper just before the race Brian Kilby from Britain, who had come 29th in Rome, discussed tactics. The article touched on the strength of Bikila but then went on to add:

In addition to Bikila, there's another Ethiopian named Mamo Wolde, whose best distance reportedly is 15 miles. Thus it's expected that the latter may set a killing pace from the starting gun in the hope of running the other leading contenders into the ground in the early stages of the race. If Wolde could do that, Bikila would figure to have little trouble winning ... But Kilby promises not to fall for such a ruse, if it is tried.

It seems as though this is almost what happened. The race began at midday on April 1ˢᵗ. It was cold and drizzling. The Ethiopians did shoot into the lead, and interestingly, bearing in mind the growing rivalry between Bikila and Mamo Wolde, it was Mamo who was ahead. Everyone noticed that both of them were wearing shoes. After the race Aurele Vandendriessche of Belgium, a 31-year-old bookkeeper who had arrived only the day before and had had trouble sleeping because of jet lag and nevertheless then won with a time of 2 hours 18 minutes 58 seconds, said: "Once the race started and I seen [sic] how the two Ethiopians ran away so fast I hoped to myself that they might over burden themselves. But, I didn't want to change my style of running – and I kept thinking about the third place."

Such was the reputation of the two Ethiopians that at six miles from the finish the Belgian said he was "startled" to even see them. "Two miles from the finish line, with people still cheering me on I passed Abebe Bikila who had beaten me [by] just 100 yards in the Olympic race at Athens. A little while after this I went by Mamo Wolde." As he passed Bikila, Vandendriessche was reported to have flashed a smile at him before waving to the crowd, blowing his nose and then breaking into a sprint.

Until then all eyes had been on Bikila and Mamo. The

New York Times gives this account of the two:

> The Ethiopians padded on, victory certain, 196 steps
> to the minute. They did not smile back at the fresh-
> faced Wellesley College girls in dirty tan raincoats,
> and could not understand the little boys who shouted:
> "Hey you in the tan underwear."
>
> At Auburndale, the Ethiopians, their cheeks sunken,
> were almost half a mile ahead of Kilby who was third.
> At Center Street in Newton, Bikila shouted something
> at Wolde, then sprinted ahead of his countryman. But
> at Brookline, Bikila's sturdy chest was heaving and his
> eyes seemed deeper in his narrow face.
>
> The Belgian began to gain and then at Coolidge Cor-
> ner, he passed Bikila. The Ethiopian soldier did not
> look at him as he flashed by.

Both of them began to slip now. Bikila was to only
come in fifth with a time of 2 hours 24 minutes 43 seconds. Mamo Wolde, clearly exhausted, came twelfth.
The American John J. Kelley came second with a time
of 2 hours 21 minutes 43 seconds and Brian Kilby came
third with 2 hours 21 minutes 43 seconds. One oddity of
the race was that with the state troopers on motorbikes,
who were ahead of the runners, were three cars from the
Massachusetts Society for the Prevention of Cruelty to
Animals. They were there to pick up stray dogs because
three years earlier a runner had tripped over one.

Without a doubt these were the years of closest cooperation and friendship between Bikila and Niskanen. The
trainer was at his peak and his pupil was still listening
to him. They still had a common goal and were prepared
to work towards it together. From 1961 onwards, Niskanen was full-time secretary-general of the Ethiopian

Red Cross Society, with which he had been associated on and off since 1948. He was also one of the founders of the Ethiopian National Athletics Federation and its vice-chairman. From 1960 to 1969, his CV also records that he was: "Official and coach of Ethiopian athletes participating in many international competitions around the world."

Basil Heatley, the English runner who was to come second to Bikila in Tokyo, remembers Niskanen from a meeting in San Sebastian. He came over to meet the Britons, have a drink with them, and also presumably size them up and find out about their training. Heatley remembers that Niskanen was "really interested in what makes the other man tick." The Englishman was also alarmed when he heard what sort of treatment Niskanen gave his runners, something that they, at that time, could only dream about: "He said the Ethiopians got physio-therapy after every session. My reaction was 'how can I compete with someone who is getting expert treatment – a personal trainer?'"

According to Alain Lunzenfichter, the Niskanen effect can be seen in the differences between the ways Bikila ran in Rome and in Tokyo. "There are two ways to run a marathon," he says, "not fifty."

> The first way is to *run to arrive*. That's what he did in Rome. He was never ahead, he did not know how to run, he was always behind until he accelerated at 41 kilometres. The second method is to *run to win* which is what he did in 1964. The idea is to get ahead and not to worry about anyone else.

On Niskanen's suggestion, Bikila took some three

months off to rest before he began his training schedule for Tokyo. This led to all sorts of gossip in Addis Ababa to the effect that the hero of Rome would not win a second time around in Japan.

Just before the games however, Bikila and Mamo Wolde filed complaints against the Ethiopian Sports Confederation for the lack of training programmes. The *Ethiopian Herald* reported on 12 July 1964 that the two runners had stated that the Sports Confederation had "remained dormant for whole years and when only 20 to 30 days are left for the Olympics, it tries to make champions out of us." The paper commented that it was shocking that funds for their training had come solely from the armed forces sports organisations. It is possible that these remarks were in fact the public face of a new row that had broken out over Niskanen, who himself complained in *Svenksbladet* that, "as usual the preparation of the Ethiopian participants in the Olympic games started too late."

Just as in the run up to Rome, a quarrel had broken out over Niskanen's participation; the Ethiopian trainers now renewed their attack with a vengeance. The Athletics Federation did not select Niskanen as an Olympic team coach and so officials of the Imperial Bodyguard told the Federation that, if this was case, not only would their runners, including Bikila, not go to train in Debre Zeit but they would not go to the Olympics either. The trainers accused the Bodyguard of favouring a foreigner. Colonel Bekele Gezaw recalls that not only was the matter taken once more to Lieutenant General Merid Mengesha, but that the Council of Ministers discussed the question for three whole days. There were several suggestions as to how to resolve the crisis and in the end the formula was devised that Niskanen would participate as an "adviser" rather than an official coach.

Tadele Yidnekatchew, the son of Yidnekatchew Tessema, remarks: "It was petty jealousies. They were simply not up to it. They had not proved themselves before nor have they done so since."

Suddenly, disaster struck. Bikila was taken ill with appendicitis. Only a few weeks earlier Niskanen himself had had to be operated on for the same thing so he recognised the symptoms. This proved a pretext for the trainers to renew their attacks.

Bikila was hit with appendicitis on 16ᵗʰ September which was 15 days before the team was due to set off for Tokyo and 40 days before the marathon itself. Bikila began to feel stabbing pains in his stomach while training in Debre Zeit. He was immediately rushed to Addis Ababa's Haile Selassie Hospital. There a German doctor, who was noted for treating the Ethiopian athletes for free, confirmed that he was suffering from an appendicitis. In consultation with Yidnekatchew and Niskanen, a midnight decision was taken that Bikila had to be operated on immediately. There was no possibility of delay. The next day an almighty row erupted. Niskanen's enemies accused him and Yidnekatchew of making a decision that had not been approved by a committee of doctors and which, even worse, was going to lose Ethiopia its chance of a gold medal in the Tokyo marathon. The Emperor convened a medical committee, which rapidly concluded that the right decision had been made.

This is Niskanen's account of what happened after the operation:

Abebe Bikila was positive and the smile and hearty handshake he gave me just after the operation meant I could return to coaching the others in Debre Zeit with a calm heart. I knew he would be at the marathon start if no post-operative complications arose. Everything went well, and after a few days when I went to see him, he was up and walking around the hospital which he left after a week ... There was no question of him training before leaving for Japan. Only walks and careful gymnastics. After arriving in Tokyo we had three weeks until the marathon.

Meanwhile, on the streets, the rumour spread that Bikila's appendicitis was divine retribution for his insistence on having a foreign trainer.

Just before the team left for Tokyo they were summoned to see the Emperor, just as they had been before Rome. They were gathered in the grounds of the Menelik palace and there was *Ambo* mineral water and Coke to drink. The Emperor told them that they had a "responsibility" to the country to win. "I hope there will be many Abebes this time, so be strong and may the Lord be with you. All the best." Inside the palace, the Emperor sat on his throne and there were many officials gathered around him. Wami Biratu says: "We were very proud to be in front of the Emperor but, of course, it was not our first time." He was summoned to see the Emperor personally and so we can assume that Bikila was too.

Before the games, Colin Gibson of *World Sports* had been to Ethiopia to watch Bikila training. His remarks published in April 1964 bear reference to some of Bikila's disappointing times since Rome:

Talking to him through an interpreter (despite his globe-trotting he only has a smattering of English) I got the impression that Bikila cares only about the Olympics and cannot be bothered to prepare himself fully for other international events. On this basis it would be dangerous to attach too much importance to any of his performances since Rome.

Since this observation proved accurate, it is also worth quoting his second point:

Bikila is first and foremost an Ethiopian with great national pride, secondly a soldier, and lastly a runner. This strange attitude is reflected in his almost complete disinterest in press-cuttings about himself, photographs or interviews ... But there can be no doubt that he is determined to win another gold medal in Japan ...

7. Tokyo

The Ethiopian team touched down in Tokyo at 6.30 am on the 29ᵗʰ of September. Journalists were already waiting at the airport to see if Bikila was there. To Niskanen's delight, the Japanese had provided the Olympians with a sauna. After a tour around Tokyo he recorded "we started training and then had a sauna and a massage."

What Bikila thought of the arrangements we do not know, but Niskanen was clearly ecstatic. He thought they were "perfect." Apart from the sauna, there was of course the Olympic village, sports halls, sports fields and space for ball sports. There was a special hospital and large food tents. There were also hundreds of new bicycles, which had been provided for the athletes to get around the village and, according to Niskanen, there was a "constant hunt for these bikes". Bikila, not used to riding one, tried one out and the experience almost ended in disaster. On the second day Bikila came in with a bandaged hand. He had fallen while bicycling. He had gone to the hospital where he had been spotted by some journalists. Terrified, Bikila had not dared ask the hospital to take care of his knee, which was more seriously hurt, and so he had hidden the injury until he could get Niskanen to look at it. In the meantime, vastly exaggerated reports of Bikila's condition were flashed around the world, prompting a telegram from Addis Ababa expressing concern. Niskanen wrote: "They had made a mountain out of a molehill. There was no more cycling for Abebe. It was bad enough getting over his appendix operation." In the days that followed there was no let up in the pressure. Bikila was a world sporting celebrity and Niskanen had to fight hard to give him space. He wrote:

> Our quarters in the Olympic village were invaded daily by journalists and photographers wanting to interview Abebe. Not only during training but even while he ate, slept or signed autographs. We were forced to hold back and restrict press visits at times. The largest Japanese TV Company NHK rang up and wanted to ensure an interview with Abebe at 7.00 pm after he had won the marathon. I must say that was being early! This happened 10 days before the race. I promised that if they were so sure Abebe would win they would get their interview, and they did.

Niskanen was not only impressed by the Japanese Olympic organisation but he was also bowled over by Tokyo, which he had not visited since the Osaka race of 1961:

> Tokyo, with its 11 million inhabitants is a fantastic city. The people are filled with a zeal for their work. In just three years since I was there, there have been great changes. New modern areas grow up where there used to be slum quarters. The traffic is fantastic. There are nearly two million cars in Tokyo and there are hardly any accidents. Everyone follows the traffic rules strictly. The Japanese Olympic organisers did a great

job by daily closing off a lane for marathon practice in the middle of this amazing traffic. Thousands of policemen watched over every little side street to make sure no traffic would disturb the runners during their training.

Despite Niskanen's upbeat mood, things did not look good in the Ethiopian camp. The athletes did creditably, but did not win any medals. Hopes began to centre on Mamo Wolde but during the 10,000 metre race he was pushed and almost fell. The incident led to a bad rip in one of his calf muscles and although he still came fourth he could hardly walk afterwards. This was disastrous because it meant he could not participate in the marathon. What Bikila thought of this we can only guess, but we can speculate that it helped relieve the pressure on him. At Debre Zeit, Bikila had beaten Mamo by one second only during the trials and Mamo had been improving constantly in training in Japan. It goes without saying that the disappointment was crushing for Mamo Wolde.

Everyone knew the marathon was still going to be tough. Since Rome the world's best time had been beaten three times. The Japanese, Toru Terasawa, had clocked 2 hours 15 minutes 15.8 seconds in 1963 and Basil Heatley had stormed to victory in the 1964 Windsor to Chiswick marathon with a time of 2 hours 13 minutes 55 seconds. He was now the holder of the world record and Niskanen knew him, having met him in San Sebastian. The Ethiopians also knew Brian Kilby who had beaten Bikila in Boston the year before. He was one of the favourites along with Heatley.

In the run up to the race, which was to take place on

123

October 21ˢᵗ, Basil Heatley recalls, "I won't say I wrote the Ethiopians off but knowing that Bikila had had appendicitis ... " There were two reasons the British were still a little cautious. Firstly, they didn't know if the appendicitis story was really true, or a lie put about to put the competition at its ease. Secondly, they had had at end of line the opportunity to size up Bikila in training - and they had been impressed. The Olympic athletics camp was a former US Army base and the athletes trained by running around its two and half mile perimeter road. Kilby recalls: "We did a fair bit around it and on a couple of occasions we ran alongside him":

> I was struck by his deep concentration. During a marathon, isolation is paramount and he had a capacity to isolate himself more than anybody. Few could have more separation from their surroundings than Abebe had and the benefits that that can bring are very marked.

As in Rome, the official film of the Olympic games is a rich source of detail. The marathon sequences begin with aerial views shot from a helicopter. It swerves over the Olympic flame and the stadium, packed to the gills with 90,000 people. It then flies up the beginning of the route, which was already jammed with eager spectators.

The Japanese officials wore blue jackets and white hats with red bands. In the film, they can be seen ushering athletes to take up their positions. There were 68 of them on the starting line. Bikila can be seen striding purposefully up to the back of the group.

He was wearing shoes and white socks. Neil Allen,

who had seen Bikila in Rome, wrote in his *Olympic Diary: Tokyo 1964*: "Here, perhaps, was a sign that this champion from an heroic age, was learning from modern sport. But Bikila explained, quite simply, 'I happened to buy them in the Olympic village.' Fittingly they were what ordinary athletes call 'warm up shoes.'"

This may be the only recorded instance of Bikila telling a lie. For this we have the record of Kihachiro Onitsuka who had made Bikila his first running shoes in 1961. He was, of course, hoping that Bikila would now wear his trainers for the Tokyo race. "Sorry", said Niskanen, "Bikila is not in a position to wear 'Tiger' shoes for the marathon. He has other commitments." They were Pumas. Onitsuka remembers: "I was a bit shocked. I understood that despite the strict rules of amateurism which prevailed at the time, a competitor had perhaps another way of doing business than I did." In other words, he suspected that Bikila was being paid by Puma, then far larger than Onitsuka's company.

Apart from the shoes, Bikila wore a black vest, sported the number 17 and wore shorts that have been described as being the colour of "dried blood."

Basil Heatley's memories are a valuable source of sporting colour, which also give us a detailed sportsman's eye-view of the race:

> There appeared to be a three-day weather cycle in Tokyo. On the first day of the games there was a torrential downpour. The next day it was extremely humid and on the third day it was very pleasant. This seemed to repeat itself and so the day of the marathon was extremely humid, over 90%, and very uncomfortable.

As we were warming up I saw sweat dripping off the neck and shoulders of Brian Kilby. I thought 'Christ! If it's like that now what's it going to be like later on?' I thought there were going to be a lot of overambitious people early on – and I was proven right!

On the film, Bikila cannot be seen as the starting gun goes. In fact, he was one of the last out of the stadium, but he soon began to close on the others.

At five kilometres, the leading group comprised the Australian, Ron Clarke, who was followed by the Irishman, Jim Hogan, the Tunisian, M. Haddeb Hannachi, and a duo of the Englishman, Ron Hill and another Tunisian, Hedhili Ben Boubaker. In the latter part of the group were Bikila, two Kenyans and an Italian. As Clarke and Hogan began to pull ahead, Bikila began to accelerate too. By the tenth kilometre, the three were running virtually side by side and it is here that the film picks up again. By the 15th kilometre, they were already more than a minute ahead of the next group, but soon Clarke began to fall back. Bikila moved ahead. At the 20th kilometre, Bikila stopped to snatch a mixture of fruit juice and glucose. Hogan, who was 25 metres behind, thought this was his chance. He closed the gap to three metres but his effort proved futile. Bikila was off again. This was the point at which he had agreed with Niskanen that he should begin to surge and it was also the point at which Niskanen was waiting. No one would catch Bikila again. Shattered, Hogan dropped out at the 35th kilometre.

Bikila hardly needed to look behind to know he was alone. Alain Lunzenfichter makes the general observation that in marathon running you can "feel" the competition behind you. "You can feel if the person is alright. You don't need to look. You do a little acceleration and then you can hear it in their breath."

Peter Wilson of the *Daily Mirror* wrote: "The heavy clouds seemed to press down on the runners like some sopping grey sponge." He dubbed Bikila, "a metronome on legs." Along the course, up to two million people had come out to watch the runners. Heatley recalled later: "I began to think I was at the Coronation." Wilson added that the effect of the noise and the race "began to have an almost hypnotic effect on runners and spectators alike." He notes:

> The Japanese thronged the roadside ten deep and more at places, crowded the balconies, swarmed up the cherry trees in the suburbs, obscured the spider-writing on the limp hanging banners. And as the factories and the flats and the flimsy-looking houses were left behind, Bikila's piston-pounding legs seemed to spell out the message: "There's no discharge in the war."

Looking at the ground about two metres in front of him and breathing with "enviable" rhythm, The *Times* of London dubbed him the "Emperor of the Road." The Japanese film is stupendous here. With the camera moving level with Bikila it switches to slow motion. Drops of sweat fall from his chin. His shoulders glisten. Suddenly he grabs some water, takes a swig, pours the rest on his head and lets the cup drop. It was only his second drink and was taken one hour and three-quarters into the race. Wilson wrote:

> There isn't, of course, an ounce of spare flesh on him

and his legs could belong to some sinewy old rooster. The face is expressionless, branded with the black bar of his moustache and topped with black crinkly hair. He has a ring on one finger.

As he approached the stadium, the cameraman shot him from the back, the Olympic flame over the stadium captured just above his shoulder. From the front, it can be seen that Bikila was quite alone now. Ron Clarke and all the rest of them had long since dropped back and out of sight. Even as he entered the stadium, to the accompaniment of trumpets, Wilson's shrewd observation that he had been expressionless remained true. The crowd roared, because they knew who he was having followed the marathon by radio broadcast into the stadium. There was no let up. His arms rose (a little) as he burst through the tape. He had won his second gold with a new world best time of 2 hours 12 minutes 11.2 seconds. He was the first person ever to win two marathon gold medals. He had made Olympic history – again.

Bikila now proceeded to baffle the Japanese officials and shock onlookers. Instead of collapsing, he immediately began going through a physical culture routine. He made as if to touch his toes twice then lay down on his back, cycling his legs in the air. He then threw his legs over his head and only then jumped up, grass on the back of his head, to finally acknowledge the crowd by throwing his arms up in the air. Bikila received the ovation of his life, while many were in hysterics because of his exercises. Primo Nebiolo, who had already seen Bikila win in Rome remarks, "we were astonished. He did these gymnastics just like you might do when you get up in the morning. He gave this impression of strength and force. He was a phenomenon." Later, Bikila explained that he had not gone through his gym routine to amuse the crowd but simply because he had cramp and felt dizzy.

As if this was not enough excitement, Kokichi Tsuburaya of Japan now entered the stadium, leading Basil Heatley. With the end in sight, Heatley began to sprint, shooting past Tsuburaya to seize the silver. The crowd rose and Allen recorded that they sighed and moaned "Oh, who will save the face of Japan?" Wilson wrote graphically that:

> As Heatley crossed the finishing line Tsuburaya, 20 yards back, began to waver and wobble like a man moving away from some shocking accident. It was the bitter disappointment rather than the fatigue which turned his knees to water and his legs to jelly ...

Bikila had beaten Heatley and Tsuburaya by more than four minutes. In the end, this humiliation on home turf was to prove calamitous for Tsuburaya. Immediately afterwards he was ordered to stop seeing his girlfriend and start training for the 1972 games in Mexico. Injuries took him to hospital and when he came out he realised that he would never be able to run as fast as he could before. He committed *hara-kiri* two years after the Tokyo games leaving a note saying simply: "I can't run anymore."

Brian Kilby came fourth clocking up a time of 2 hours 17 minutes 2.4 seconds.

Heatley's account of the race is fascinating and this part of his interview is worth recording in full. Re-

member that Heatley had already been alarmed by the
humidity and guessed that too many people would try
and run too fast too quickly:

Bikila started off behind and then, as he passed me,
I thought: "Oh yes, here he is." For all I knew the
story about the operation hadn't been true. Anyway
he knew exactly what he was doing. He was just a
natural racing machine.

My idea was to stay back and move up. I could see
that a lot of people were going far too fast. There were
a lot ahead of me so at halfway I thought 'I've blown
it.' But then, a lot dropped out – they had overrun it
in those conditions. At 15 miles I was running parallel
with Brian (Kilby) so I knew if I was with him I was
going fast enough.

After 20 miles I could see the Hungarian Jozsef
Suto and Tsuburaya ahead of me. I didn't know if they
were leading and I assumed there were several ahead
of them. Then they separated and Suto fell back. Then
I left Brian and overtook Suto and then realised that
Tsuburaya was coming back – that's our term for catching up with someone. As I approached the stadium I
didn't know what the situation was, I just knew that it
was beginning to look like a sprint finish. As I entered
the stadium there was a deafening noise. It was because, until then, Japan hadn't got an athletics medal.
It was 90,000 Japanese shouting 'hooray' – but I knew
the gap was lessening. The distance between us stayed
the same for most of the back straight then I started to
sprint. I changed gear for about 100 yards. I changed
it from a 20 yard deficit into a 10 yard advantage and,
well, Tsuburaya was gutted. My sprint was instinctive.
I knew 'now is the time.' The conscious part was not
to show my hand too soon. It was to hit hard – and
late, when he had no chance of catching up again.

I knew I was well up there but I didn't know where
I'd come until one of my colleagues rushed out with

my thermos of tea. I wasn't in much of a state actually and then I was led off by the Japanese officials. When the Japanese have arranged something their officials make sure their orders are carried out. I was taken to a recovery room and half an hour later we were led out to the awards ceremony.

That evening I went to Bikila's accommodation but he and Niskanen were being led out, perhaps going to do some TV. I just had the chance to wave.

When Bikila came to receive his medal the Japanese band did not know the Ethiopian national anthem so they played their own one instead.

Bikila said that he had been "200 percent certain" that he would win by the time he got to the halfway mark. Niskanen added: "Once the doctors had told me he would be fit in time after his operation I knew there could only be one winner." Bikila, on top of the world, went on to predict that he was going to make it a hat-trick: "I shall train on for the next Olympics in 1968 and I expect to win easily in Mexico City. After all, I shall have the advantage because it is 7,000 feet high just like the country where I train."

Writing in *Svenksbladet*, the Swedish Community newspaper in Addis Ababa, in December 1964, Niskanen recorded the headlines of three world papers writing about Bikila's victory:

PALACE GUARD ON THE THRONE
Abebe Bikila's Second Marathon One-Man Show Puts Him In Greatness
Abebe Bikila, pride and joy of Haile Selassie's Imperial Guard in Ethiopia, became a great this afternoon when he outran 67 of the world's best long-distance

runners to make a one-man show of the Tokyo Olympics marathon.

ABEBE WINS MARATHON AGAIN

Ethiopia's phenomenal iron-legged, stout-hearted Abebe Bikila made Olympic history on Wednesday by becoming the first man to win the marathon, the blue ribbon event of the Olympic Games, for the second time. Abebe's victory was doubly remarkable considering the fact that he had undergone an appendectomy only 40 days ago.

THE MASTER'S RACE

What a wonderful runner this Abebe Bikila. A feather-light full-blood, a racehorse with seemingly unending force. A marathon runner of unusual brightness. Bikila's race was worthy of a master ... Not a second's doubt about taking the lead and command. Seemingly untouched he kept his speed that no one else could bear to keep up. Obviously Bikila had not had time for morning gymnastics! After the triumphant entrance into the Olympic stadium he cut the winning tape and then made up for it!

Later Bikila claimed (in a blatantly grotesque piece of false modesty, that the happiest day of his life had nothing to do with winning the race. The real reason was that, after winning the race, he lost his gold wedding ring in the shower. A day later reported the *Ethiopian Herald*: "a Tokyo housewife cleaning the athlete's showers handed to the Olympics Organising Committee the ring she had found." Almost certainly his real emotion was one of relief.

Bikila's return to Addis Ababa was no less triumphant than the one that had taken place four years before. Tens of thousands turned out to cheer him on his victorious ride into the city. He waved with both hands, shook hands with many in the crowd and received innumerable bouquets of flowers. This time a lorry had been adapted so that the garlanded Bikila emerged from out of a large, painted globe, a map of Africa to the fore. The front of the lorry was painted with two flaming Olympic torches and in the centre was the coat of arms of the Imperial Bodyguard.

As in 1960, he was driven straight to the royal palace. Here Haile Selassie pinned on him the Order of Menelik II. He promoted him to lieutenant, awarded him his own private Volkswagen and house and said that the success he had scored had been due to the "help of the Almighty." He also praised Mamo Wolde.

Following the ceremony, there was a reception given by the chief of the Imperial Bodyguard. The newspapers talked of the relief felt all over the country that Bikila had won the second time around and the *Ethiopian Herald* opined that: "There are hundreds of Abebes in Ethiopia whose potential abilities either remain undiscovered or overlooked."

There is a picture of Bikila printed on the same day, which shows him holding a painting, which has just been given to him. He looks uncertain. The picture appears to show a man with a spear on a flying horse, but the caption reads: "The art shows a human's heart, an elephant's strength and a horse's leg focusing the world's attention on the Ethiopian flag."

8. Downhill to Mexico

Bikila was not just an Ethiopian hero now but a pan-African one too. A poll in *Jeune Afrique* magazine, which is sold all over Francophone Africa, found that he was the most popular person in Africa. He was also the most popular man in Addis Ababa.

Bikila was the toast of the town. "Slender, handsome and resplendent in plumed helmet and beribboned red coat of the Imperial Guard," gushed an article in the *New York Times* in March 1965, "Bikila walks the streets as a national hero." It went on: "He now lives the life of a celebrity and a rich man ... He moves in the highest society. He has everything he wants."

Men wanted to be seen with him. They invited him for drinks, for dinner and to their home. It was prestigious to be spotted in his company – a little of his fame might rub off onto you. As for women, the man now had star quality and hence star attractions. Bikila revelled in the fame, but it was to have disastrous consequences. His hitherto mild drinking and discreet womanising took off. This is the account of someone whose aunt had an affair with him:

She was the owner of a restaurant and very attractive. She was in her thirties and divorced. He would come and spend the whole night drinking whisky. Then they would go off somewhere. Once they had a car accident. He drove into a wall. She was cut but not badly hurt. In her restaurant she had a record player and they would play the music of Tilahun Gessese. Lots of high officials came to her restaurant but she refused to sleep with them and so he stayed with her.

Tilahun Gessese was, of course, Bikila's friend who he had rescued from detention after the failed coup of 1960. Later, Bikila's friends would go to great lengths to insist that he was only really interested in sport, that he drank *Ambo* mineral water, or possibly Coke, and that in general he was a saint. Of course, this is not the real picture. Bikila loved being feted and fame went to his head. Until Tokyo though the malign side effects of this were kept under control. Now he lost his self-restraint. According to trainer Belete Ergetie, "he became a different person."

> He was affected by fame. Before Tokyo he may have had some relations with women but now it gradually became open. He was found drunk many times – and almost everywhere around town. It was sad – the whole nation was concerned.

Roman Reta, Niskanen's cook, remembers that in private Niskanen told off both Bikila and Mamo Wolde, ordering them to ease off on the drink. They would both agree, but clearly in Bikila's case, these warnings made little difference. Tadele Yidnekatchew believes that his father almost certainly talked to Bikila too, but says that he would only have done so extremely discreetly. As for the womanising, Tadele says that Bikila's wife certainly knew about it but, in keeping with her simple background and the tradition of subservient Ethiopian wives, would most likely have suffered in silence.

Whatever the gossip about Bikila around town, none of this leaked out into the strictly controlled local press or the foreign media. Indeed, whether managed by Niskanen or not, the story that was being told abroad was the one, as the *New York Times* put it, of the "devoted family man". It said:

> According to family tradition, he is still obedient to his mother at the age of 32, almost like a small child. He doesn't sit or smoke in her presence without her authorization. He cannot enter a room unless his mother says it's all right.

One difference from before was that Bikila now had some money of his own. We know that it is most likely that he had received a payment from Puma but he also had a regular income from the house the Emperor had given him after Tokyo. The two to three bedroom home had been built by the Swedes in the compound of their Building College. The Emperor had bought it for Bikila and he in turn rented it back to the Swedes who needed houses for their aid workers.

At the time, the man in charge of accommodation was Roland Axelsson. He says that the Emperor had not "given" the house to Bikila, perhaps because this would have contravened the prevailing spirit of sporting amateurism, but rather presented it to him as a "payment for good work." Bikila would come every quarter to collect his money, at first accompanied by Niskanen, who presumably had fixed up the rental in the first place, then later by himself.

Axelsson remembers Bikila as being "very quiet", a confirmation of the fact that the man had two faces, one for Europeans and one for the Ethiopians with whom he felt more comfortable.

Although a large slice of Addis Ababa society was in awe of Bikila, some people were not. The upper classes and the ruling elite of the country were far less impressed by the man than those of similar backgrounds to himself. Firstly, despite his success, he was, after all, an Oromo peasant. When it came to Bikila, fathers from the upper classes were not only keen to preserve the honour of their daughters, but especially so given his humble origins, which were betrayed every time he opened his mouth. Running in Ethiopia also had no social status, or rather the problem was it did. It was associated with servitude. While masters rode their horses, it was their slaves and servants who ran along behind them.

Although, of course, the Emperor was pleased by Bikila's success, he too eventually began to find it irksome. Tafari Wossen is now an urbane and sophisticated filmmaker and journalist, but in the early 1970s, he worked in the government's press department. He recalls that the Emperor and his circle were put out by the way that, in terms of foreign associations of Ethiopia, lowborn Bikila was beginning to eclipse even the sovereign himself.

In *Svenskbladet*, in November 1964, Niskanen wrote that: "Abebe Bikila and Mamo Wolde are the two Ethiopian athletes who have made Ethiopia famous worldwide." This was exactly the type of statement, which would have annoyed the Emperor and his entourage. But there was worse. In March 1965, a story by the *Associated Press* said: "Only the Emperor Haile Selassie has greater stature among his people – and not much." The story noted that Bikila "lives the life of the king – not just a king's bodyguard."

There were others, closer to Bikila, who were also beginning to find the man irritating – and increasingly arrogant. He pulled rank, making sure that fellow Guardsmen knew he was an officer now. When he was outside, people would cheer him.

Tsige Abebe's book understandably paints her father in the best possible light, but she does write that senior officers began to "secretly entertain annoyance, accusing him of being one who did whatever he liked." In the officers' mess, or if there was a tennis match, he rarely gave up his seat for one them. A star, he was becoming untouchable. But that is not to say that Bikila had no concerns. He did. He was unnerved by Mamo Wolde, whom he feared was coming up behind him, ready at any moment to seize his crown.

In the meantime, Bikila still played football and, once on the pitch, would become extremely aggressive. "He who received Abebe's hard tackles," writes Tsige Abebe, "often got severe injuries. Regular members of the football sports group ... used to be filled with fear when playing with Abebe." The implication is clear. They were frightened that if they gave as good as they got then they would risk severe punishment if they happened to injure the national treasure.

At "work", Bikila had little to do. He received mountains of letters from across the world, including requests for autographed photos. He leafed through magazines and newspapers and received foreign correspondents and other visitors. These included tourists, sports coaches and photographers. Most importantly perhaps, he made frequent trips around the country and abroad, speaking to sportsmen and children and generally playing an inspirational role. None who met the man forgot him.

After Tokyo though, and before the Mexico City games of 1968, Bikila, while more than happy to bask in glory, shone rather less than before. He competed frequently in Japan however, and to this day he is fondly remembered there. He also made other foreign trips.

In April 1965, Bikila and Mamo were invited to New York to take part in the World Fair. They were to run as part of the opening ceremonies and carry a parchment scroll from the Emperor to the Queens Borough President, Mario Cariello, and fair officials. Bikila was described by the *New York Times* as "lithe", who quoted him as saying: "I am here for one purpose only ... that is to run for the fair." This was perhaps in response to a question about whether he was to take part in the Boston marathon again, which was to be held a few days later. Apart from running, he said he had "no special plans" but was "very anxious to see a baseball game". Bikila also went on to predict that he would win the marathon in Mexico:

> "I am very confident," he said, with a wide grin, "that I will be champion there, providing God Almighty is willing. I do my best and I keep practising as much as 5 to 10 miles a day."

Perhaps it was not enough, or rather it might have been had it not also been for the changes in his lifestyle. In retrospect, Tafari Wossen believes that Bikila thought that his success was innate, something "in the blood". He did not understand that "discipline was necessary". In fact, this fault may not have been Bikila's alone but that of a whole generation of athletes. Tafari Wossen says that Bikila came from the elite of what was then one of the best-trained armies in Africa. "They did not maintain the pressure because they did not understand."

Today, it is widely believed in Ethiopia that the track stars of the present and recent past, such as marathon runners Haile Gebreselassie and Fatuma Roba, the 1996 Atlanta Olympics women's champion, maintain their success and training because they have learned from the experience of pioneers like Bikila. But, Ottavio Castellini, the Italian marathon historian, says that even today, there are many that have not. Alcohol abuse remains a major problem amongst east African long distance runners.

Still, it would be unfair to imply that Bikila gave up training. Unless he was exaggerating, he told the *Associated Press* that he would run ten miles in the morning and then rest in the afternoon. The next day he would do physical training and gym and then the day after that he would run another ten or fifteen miles. Then he said he would play basketball, volleyball and tennis for about two hours before running again. Referring to Mexico he said: "Nobody can beat me for some time to come."

In March 1967, the *New York Times* ran another feature about Bikila. "Of course I will win in Mexico," he told the reporter, Eric Pace. Interestingly he added,

"When I run I do not even see my competitors, I only see a car [carrying reporters] following me." Niskanen, who was present, and described as "burly", chipped in that Bikila would not be able to run as fast in Mexico because of the altitude of 7,400 feet but then added that since Addis Ababa was at an altitude of 8,000, his man would have a "comparative advantage" over others.

As in the previous piece from two years earlier, Bikila was painted as a rather saintly family man who spent his evenings, "lazily enough ... He hangs up his beige pith helmet and eats a simple supper – with plenty of meat – cooked by his wife Yewbdar." There was no mention of late night carousing here and, indeed, according to the piece, Bikila liked nothing more than to watch "Sudanese arias" on television with a cup of tea or "very occasionally" a glass of beer.

> But the mornings are different. Then he is out of bed by six, slips on his green sweatsuit, and takes off without breakfast for an hour or so of running through the hills around Addis Ababa. After covering about 10 miles without getting out of breath, he changes into uniform, and pith helmet and reports for duty.
>
> "Training is important," Abebe says in his matter-of-fact fashion. "If someone else wins at Mexico City, it just means that that person did more training than I did."

On reflection though, Bikila added that while practising was up to him, "victory comes from God." Later, in what we can now see as a cruelly ironic twist, Bikila said that he had not decided whether or not to retire after Mexico.

"Maybe after Mexico I'll start drinking [hard liquor]," he said with a small and slightly thirsty-looking grin. "After that with my age I don't think I'll be so active, so it won't matter much."

The run up to the Mexico Olympics was troubled, both for Bikila and for the games themselves. First, there was the threat of an African boycott, a move led by Ethiopia, because of the then apartheid South Africa's participation. This was lifted once South Africa was banned. The Soviet invasion of Czechoslovakia provoked the threat of a Nordic boycott, but it was not carried out. Then fighting broke out between Mexican students and police.

Bikila himself had been troubled for almost a year with leg or knee problems. From July 1967, four months after the upbeat article by Eric Pace, he had begun to limp, apparently because of recurring hamstring troubles. According to Colonel Bekele Gezaw yet another problem had arisen in Athens during an international armed services competition. Bikila tried to minimise it to Niskanen, saying that his massages would help it to go away. They did not. Four months before the games were due to begin, Bikila was forced to take a month off from training. When the news reached the Emperor he ordered that he be despatched to a top hospital in Germany. It was July 1968 and Bikila was given $6,000 to cover costs. Because the patient was Bikila the German government refused the money and, on his return, the Emperor decided to let him keep it. However, the visit to Germany did not cure the problem.

The Ethiopian Olympic team, which was to go to

Mexico, was the largest ever. There were 11 runners, five boxers, five cyclists, five coaches and officials. One month's training at Debre Zeit was followed by one month in Asmara, which is at the same altitude as Mexico City (2,200 metres) and has a similar hot climate. Bikila got back to Ethiopia in time to go to Asmara but, according to Niskanen, "still had pains in his leg." Training started slowly.

On arrival in Mexico, Bikila ran through the streets of the capital encouraged by people who saw him. He started to get better. The strain was immense though. Not only did the whole of Ethiopia expect him to win but, in stark contrast to Rome, much of the rest of the world now did too. Probably Bikila was egged on by another factor. Niskanen and the other Ethiopian officials in Mexico were drilling Mamo Wolde with the idea that he must take up the baton for Ethiopia. In other words, Niskanen and the others already knew that Bikila had no chance. Niskanen admitted as much when he wrote later that Mamo Wolde had to miss another race because he had a bruise on his left toe and had to be fit to run the marathon three days later. "This was a lot," he remarked in *Svenksbladet* in February 1969, "knowing that Abebe Bikila was hurt and Mamo had to defend Ethiopian honour on this distance."

According to Belete Ergetie, Niskanen, worried by Bikila's decline, had begun to concentrate more on Mamo Wolde after Tokyo, although there would never be the closeness between them as there had once been between him and Bikila. Echoing this, Tadele Yidnekatchew says that, by the time of the Mexico games, Niskanen, "had lost his total control over Bikila."

I don't think he would listen to him after Tokyo. He became very big- headed. Niskanen was happier then with Mamo Wolde who was more obedient, more of a "robotic athlete" if you like. Even he started abusing alcohol though, but that was not until much later.

Niskanen records that when the team arrived in Mexico, "there was great unrest between students and the military police. It was no small fight, but war in the streets at night with a lot of deaths." The Olympics were due to start on October 12th but a question mark hung over the whole games after soldiers killed anywhere up to 325 protestors using machine guns and bayonets on the night of October 2nd in the Plaza del las Tres Culturas, which was situated in the new housing estate of Tlatelolco. Some of them had been chanting: "We don't want Olympic games, we want revolution!" The French journalists, Guy Lagorce and Robert Parienté, reported on the aftermath: "Everywhere there were puddles of blood and even bits of skull and scraps of brain." Hurried meetings were called between the International Olympic Committee and the Mexican government. The outcome was a decision that the games must go on.

One week before the marathon, Bikila began complaining about pains in his right calf and a stretched muscle. A Swedish doctor, whom Niskanen knew and who had looked after Mamo Wolde in Tokyo, was consulted. Niskanen wrote: "He said the sprained muscle would get better in a few days, but was more concerned about the pain and suggested X-rays." His fear proved well founded. Bikila had a cracked bone, which Niskanen

characterised as an "old" crack and added, "had this
been detected whilst in Germany they might have got it
in time." The news agencies flashed around the world
that he had an "incipient fracture of the fibula bone in
the left leg and periostitis [inflammation] of the tissue
around the bone."

According to Fekrou Kidane, who later worked for
the International Olympic Committee but was then
in Mexico as the secretary-general of the Ethiopian
Olympic Committee, Bikila was also taken to see both
a French and a Mexican doctor. They agreed with the
Swedish doctor that he could race but, until the day,
he had to be confined to bed. Bikila defied their orders.
Perhaps it was the strain of seeing Mamo Wolde and
the others going out to train. But he had to be discreet.
Kidane says that the team managers only realised what
was happening when Bikila was seen sneaking out to run
– at 3 o'clock in the morning. The pressure was certainly
increased when Mamo Wolde won the silver in the th-
rilling 10,000 metre final. Niskanen must have been full
of it. Later he recorded the event, still brimming with
enthusiasm:

> Mamo Wolde was in good form ... It was agreed
> that he should stay in the lead group until 20 laps were
> done and then he was to give it his all. Everything
> went according to plan and then when there were five
> laps to go he speeded up. The other good runners were
> immediately left behind. Only [Naftali] Temu from Ke-
> nya speeded up all he could. These two, Mamo about
> 25 metres ahead, kept up the same tough pace for the
> remaining laps. Temu got closer and closer. When the
> bell rang for the last lap Mamo went up to his maxi-
> mum speed, and so did Temu. One hundred metres

before the goal Temu was only a few metres behind. Both gave all they had, Temu just a few steps behind Mamo. The audience was ecstatic to see such a finale to the 10,000 metres race. Temu got closer, centimetre by centimetre and just before passing the goal he passed Mamo by a few centimetres.

Those few centimetres took less than half a second. On the day of the marathon, October 20th, Niskanen wrote that Bikila "was in pain and hobbling about like an old man." He was still determined to compete though. He looked terrible. From the film, it can be seen that he looked drained and tense. To make matters worse the Mexicans had honoured him by making him number "1". The race began by the cathedral of Mexico City. It was hot and humid. Niskanen wrote:

> All three Ethiopians took it easy in the beginning, but after five kilometres Abebe was in the lead group. Mamo was slightly behind with Merawi Gebru, the third Ethiopian. Ten kilometres passed with Abebe still in the lead group. At 15 kilometres he had fallen back a little, I saw he was in pain due to his leg, and I advised him to withdraw, which he did after a few kilometres. Mamo Wolde, who had been lying in the back until now, advanced slowly towards the lead. At 25 kilometres he was in third place with Temu from Kenya in the lead. He took the lead and gradually left the others behind, securing himself the Olympic gold medal.

In the *New York Times* published on the day of the race, Niskanen is quoted as saying before they left that the plan was in fact for the three Ethiopians to "take it easy at first" but that later they were supposed to run together. Negussie Roba, who was described as his Ethiopian co-coach, said: "You can never know if they will stay together. But you have to be optimistic." Some 50,000 police and troops held the crowd back, reported the paper, which described the route as twisting,

> ... through fancy residential areas, business districts and broad palm-lined boulevards dotted with magnificent fountains. There were no hills to torture the marathoners, but the sun beat down out of a relatively cloudless sky.
>
> "The sun will get them," said Alf Cotton, the British coach, as he watched 15 tightly bunched leaders battle through the first ten miles.
>
> Of Wolde, Cotton said, "He ran a sensible race. He was up there early. But he wasn't pressing like some of the others. He took his time and moved out when he was ready."

In Tsige Abebe's account, she describes how before the race her father became ever more anxious. "A sense of defeat that he had been unwilling to accept all along now loomed over his head."

> In ... previous years his strong legs and his equally enduring spirit had coupled to move in unison to record repeated victories. Today, however, those legs couldn't sustain the endurance of the spirit. Just as suddenly, the pain became unbearable. However much he tried to shove the feeling of pain to the back of his mind, the injury worsened, continually reminding him of the pain he was trying to forget. The pain throbbed and throbbed, clearly hindering him from achieving his one goal ... It was a moment of reckoning when, at the fifteen kilometre mark, the pain in his legs became so excruciating that he became unconscious and

literally fell out of the race. When he fell he incurred a moderate injury on his hands and legs. With the aid of health officers he was taken to hospital.

Bikila should not have been walking, let alone running a marathon.

There is a point in the Olympic film in which the commentator says: "These are the last pictures of Abebe Bikila ..." The impression given by the way the film is cut is that Mamo Wolde has already passed. If Niskanen's account is right though, Mamo was still hanging back and would only have passed Bikila *after* he had dropped out. If this is the case then it gives credence to the story that, in an emotionally charged moment, Bikila, sitting by the side of the course, called out to him: "Be strong and win" as he passed. It must have been the most difficult moment of Bikila's life to date. But it was nothing compared to the pain and difficulties yet to come.

Mamo Wolde's time was 2 hours 20 minutes 26.4 seconds. It was good – but nothing like Bikila's best. Still, it was more than three minutes off Kenji Kimihara of Japan who came second to Mamo. Michael Ryan of New Zealand took the bronze. The third Ethiopian in the race, Merawi Gebru, came sixth. Mamo returned home victorious.

The relationship between Bikila and Mamo Wolde can be described as complex at best. Mamo Wolde began his Olympic career before Bikila, having participated in the 1956 games in Melbourne. He ended it in Munich in 1972, where he won a bronze medal for the marathon. This race Bikila was forced to watch from the sidelines because he was already paralysed and in a wheelchair.

Oddly, Mamo said later that: "Abebe Bikila made me want to run. He was my guiding light." This is odd, because Bikila actually decided that he wanted to run on seeing the athletes who had returned from Melbourne.

Today, there are two opinions as to their relationship. One holds that they were always good friends and that there was no rivalry, especially because they actually competed against one another in marathons comparatively few times. The other view holds that Bikila was long nervous that Mamo Wolde would knock him off his perch as Ethiopia's greatest living sporting hero.

Woldemeskal Kostre, now Ethiopia's chief athletics coach, says that when Bikila and Mamo Wolde raced or trained together Bikila would gesture at his rival, swinging his arm and shouting, "Get back Mamo!" Kostre says that, in sporting terms, where Bikila was more aggressive, Mamo Wolde had more talent. He also remembers that the two quarrelled and that relations between them had deteriorated so much before Mexico that they would no longer train together. Wami Biratu also says there was "bad feeling" between the two. Still, Mamo in victory does appear to have been extraordinarily magnanimous. Immediately after winning he said, in a remark quoted in the *New York Times* "He was not well ... If he was well I could not have beaten him."

Marathon historian, Ottavio Castellini, has worked extensively with African, and especially Kenyan, long distance runners. His observation is that while athletes can be friends off the track the minute they are either in training or actually competing "it's war". He puts this down to the East African "warrior spirit" and says that their on track competitiveness bears no relation to anything comparable to that amongst Europeans or others.

In fact, what probably happened is that their relationship changed, or went through several phases. At first, according to Belete Ergetie, they were good friends – off the track. In this he confirms Castellini's theory. However, it seems that, as the sixties wore on, their friendship deteriorated. Remember that in the final heats at Debre Zeit, before Tokyo, Bikila had only managed to beat Mamo Wolde *by one second*, and that it was then only bad luck which prevented Mamo from competing against him. Belete says that the fact that they grew to dislike each other became "the talk of the town." While Mexico may have been a crushing humiliation for Bikila, it then seems that there was something of a reconciliation. At the ill-fated, terror struck Munich games of 1972, which Bikila attended in his wheelchair, he encouraged his colleagues, including Mamo, telling them to win for Ethiopia.

Unfortunately, the pictures of the two together give us little clue as to how they felt about each other. Most of them show them both smiling. There is one exception though. It is the picture that shows them returning to Addis Ababa after Mexico. Mamo Wolde is loaded down with garlands and is holding hands with a delighted and beaming Yidnekatchew Tessema, who led the delegation, just as he had to Rome and Tokyo. Mamo Wolde looks surprisingly grim-faced. Behind him is Bikila walking with the aid of a stick. Downcast, he appears to be explaining something to someone. With only his eyes and nose visible Niskanen is there too, the *eminence grise* of Ethiopian sports, suitably hidden in the background.

The relationship between the two men was clearly a central one in Bikila's life. Just as his relationship with Niskanen was a formative one, his relations with Mamo spurred him on in a different way. From 1993 to 2002, just a few months before he died Mamo languished in jail accused of having taken part in an execution during the murderous period of the Red Terror, which took place during the regime of Mengistu Haile Mariam, who succeeded the Emperor. Mamo denied the accusation. However, his incarceration robbed him of an opportunity to tell me his story and that of his relationship with Bikila.

Tadele Yidnekatchew, Tessema's son, says that in many ways, Bikila's leg injury was a convenient excuse. He says that all athletes need one when they can no longer perform as they used to: "We knew that Bikila was not going to win in Mexico. His lifestyle had simply changed too much."

> He was drinking five or six glasses of whisky a night. When he started he was running 20 kilometres a day and then having to walk everywhere on top of that. Now he drove everywhere. In Tokyo he was still young enough to recover but by Mexico there was deterioration.

Bikila returned home and, despite his failure, he was promoted again, this time to the rank of captain. After Mamo's victory, Niskanen wrote in *Svenskbladet* in February 1969, the following curiously cool comment, perhaps reflecting his own disenchantment with his erstwhile champion. "There was joy and celebration in the Ethiopian camp ..."

At the same time as being sorry for Abebe's bad luck I was very happy for Mamo's success. One can liken it to – The King is dead. Long live the King – But, no one should think Abebe's marathon days are over. After a time of rest to cure his leg he will start training again and I wouldn't be surprised if he's at the start of the marathon at the Olympic Games in Munich in 1972.

Bikila himself said that he wanted to win again in Munich, but it was not to be.

9. Endings

On the morning of his accident on Sunday, 22 March 1969, Bikila and Wami Biratu trained together at the great *Jan Meda* field opposite the Imperial Guard head-quarters. After that, they played tennis and then drank an *Ambo* mineral water together with another friend. Bikila announced that he wanted to go to Menz, the region where his mother came from and he wanted this friend to come too. In the car, as Bikila drove Biratu home, he quarrelled with the friend, who decided he did not want to come. In the end Bikila left alone.

On his way back he was spotted in Debre Berhan, in a bar, at 9.00 pm. Later, on a wet road, 55 kilometres from Addis Ababa, something happened. Bikila's Volkswagen turned over, trapping him inside.[1] He was found early the next morning when the first bus from Debre Berhan went past. He was immediately taken to the Imperial Bodyguard Hospital in Addis Ababa.

Bikila's friend, the runner Hailu Abebe, visited him in hospital. He recalls that he was in a coma for four days, though Tsige Abebe says he was unconscious for only four hours after he arrived in hospital. When he came

---

1. *The crash distance from Addis Ababa is given as 70 or 75 kilometres in other accounts*

153

round he told Hailu that he had crashed while swerving to avoid a fast, oncoming car. This is the account he gave, which is in Tsige's book:

> When I was about to reach a small bridge over a brook, a land rover was coming from the opposite direction with its headlights on high beam. The speed at which it was coming was incredibly high. I tried to warn the driver by switching from high beam to low. However, when the land rover kept on speeding on the wrong side of the street, coming straight at me, I tried to ward off a headlong crash by steering to the side of the street, and that is when my car overturned.[2] I was unconscious of whatever happened after that.

Wami Biratu and Hailu Abebe both dismiss the notion that there was anything suspicious about the accident. Probably they are right. Maybe the account in Tsige's book is completely accurate, or maybe he had had too much to drink. We shall never know. Nevertheless, rumours spread like wildfire. The gist of them was that an attempt had been made on the life of Bikila by a wronged and jealous husband. There were also stories that the car crash was a cover up and that Bikila had in fact been shot. Needless to say, there is no proof of any of this, but the fact that these stories were widely believed says something about Bikila's reputation.

Some days after the accident, Dr Kurt Weithaler, the Austrian medical director of the Imperial Bodyguard hospital, announced that the athlete had dislocated his seventh vertebra. He may have been trying to play down the severity of the injury. Bikila would never walk again.

---

2. For "street" read "road".

For the first two months after the accident he could not even move his head and neck.

On the third day, Bikila was visited in hospital by the Emperor and Yidnekatchew Tessema. The Emperor gave orders that he should be taken to England. Fekrou Kidane says that on leaving the hospital Haile Selassie and Yidnekatchew walked through the streets together for some five or six kilometres. This was, apparently, not such an uncommon thing for the Emperor to do. Kidane says that he was in a reflective mood. He said that if Bikila had not been a champion he would not have had a car and hence would not be in hospital now.

At 6.15 in the morning on 29th March, Bikila left Addis Ababa, on the orders of the Emperor, for Stoke Mandeville Hospital in Britain, the country's most prestigious institution for treating paraplegics. Film footage from the time shows a broken man. Niskanen hastened to visit. Again rumours began to fly around Addis Ababa. This time they claimed that Bikila was dead. So Niskanen recorded Bikila's voice and, on his return to the Ethiopian capital, the tape was played on the radio to kill off such speculation.

Soon after his arrival, doctors at Stoke Mandeville pronounced that Bikila was a "model patient". They added that he had some movement in both arms and slight hand movement. But Bikila's injuries were so severe that he had to be put in a bed which had specially installed machinery to turn him every two hours. A few days after his arrival, the *Ethiopian Herald* reported the true extent of his injuries; a broken neck and "severe spinal injuries".

Bikila spent eight months in Stoke Mandeville. He was

a celebrity patient. He was paid a visit by the Queen. When Fekrou Kidane visited with Yidnekatchew Tessema, he remembers that there were about 300 to 400 letters and "get well soon" cards in the room. "I picked one up and it was from President Nixon. I also read him one from General Gowon of Nigeria."

Bikila returned home on 1 December 1969. There was nothing more that could be done for him in England. A few days before he left he announced that he intended to drive again, leading to optimistic speculation that he would need a car with specially adapted controls. On his return he received a warm welcome at the airport and waved to a waiting crowd. "Though they were there to welcome him," writes Tsige Abebe, "they couldn't help but cry or express their sadness in grim silence." She also writes that, overcome with emotion and remembering his past triumphant returns, Bikila himself bowed his head and began to cry.

For a year, Bikila lived in special rooms in the Imperial Bodyguard hospital. Although the doctors knew that he would never walk again, he still refused to accept the inevitable. Niskanen, who was now Executive Director of ALERT, the All Africa Leprosy and Rehabilitation Centre, got one of the Swedish physiotherapists who was working for him to go to the hospital twice a week to treat Bikila. Her name was Margareta Enghardt. Almost thirty years later she had this recollection of that difficult time:

> I knew he would not walk again, because the lesions on his spine were very high. But he wanted to walk. Because he had a strong religious faith he thought he would have a miracle. Wearing callipers he could

stand on his legs but only within parallel bars. He simply could not envisage his life in a wheelchair. In fact he should have put his energy into that, and prayed for that. But he did not. He had to be pushed everywhere and helped to get on the loo seat. He could eat though, but still, he was very dependent on others. Mind you if he'd been in Sweden of course it would have been much easier.

After a year, Bikila went home to live with his wife, Yewebdar, and their four young children. His appearance changed. He grew a beard and put on a considerable amount of weight. Margareta Enghardt visited him at home. "He was sweet," she recalls, but "he was very unhappy, very depressed, he just couldn't cope with it."

In 1971, Guy Lagorce from *L'Equipe*, who had met Bikila in Rome in 1960 when he had been an athlete too, (and who had also been in Mexico) travelled to Ethiopia to interview him. This is what Bikila told him:

> It was not easy for me to get used to the idea that I would never be able to run or walk again. In fact, I've never been able to get used to it because I think that, in the end, only the Lord knows what will happen to me. The doctors tell me they have little hope, in fact they have none. I'll only walk again if the Lord wills it. Men can do nothing more for me. In the beginning I thought that what had happened to me was a terrible injustice. Then, thinking about it, I thought after all, during the time that I was fit, life had given a lot to me. I had lots of luck and glory and the time that I had standing I lived to the full. My immobility is a trial that is difficult to support. I am certain that if I did not believe in the Lord I would not have the courage to survive. Every day is a real struggle. Much more difficult than the marathon. And I lead it without witnesses and without glory.

While his legs never recovered, it is clear that, at least to a certain extent, his willpower did. At home he continued the exercises he had learned at Stoke Mandeville. In July 1970, he competed in archery and table tennis in the 19th Stoke Mandeville Games for Wheelchair Sportsmen. This was a forerunner of the paralympics. In April 1971, he was invited to the disabled games being held in Norway. Bikila had actually been asked as a spectator but once he got there he declared his intention of taking part. He participated in the archery contests and table tennis and, most dramatically of all, in the sleigh-riding competition in which, amazingly, he came first out of a field of 16, completing the course in 1 hour 16 minutes 17 seconds. There is a photo of him smiling, wrapped up warmly, holding the dog which presumably pulled him to victory. He stayed a month in Norway, visiting various sites and was even received by the King himself.

Back in Ethiopia, the United States funded a gymnasium, which was built and named in his honour. Bikila insisted that it should have disabled facilities. He also played a role in the country's disabled sports federation.

In 1972, he was invited as a guest of honour to the Munich Olympics. He received a standing ovation from spectators when he entered the stadium on the opening day. He was also visited in his hotel by Chancellor Willy Brandt. Robert Parienté of *L'Equipe*, who had seen Bikila in Rome, observed: "He was like one of the Three Kings, frozen in his wheelchair. What was most striking was the great noblesse of his bearing." Kihachiro Onitsuka, who had made his first shoes, also saw him and says almost the same thing: "He maintained the image of a philosopher."

One year later, on 25 October 1973, Bikila died of a brain haemorrhage, a complication arising from his accident. Two days earlier he had complained about pains in stomach and then, says Tsige Abebe, "he was made to lie down and relax. Immediately thereafter he closed his eyes, as if falling asleep." He was rushed to hospital. There he was visited by the Emperor who gave instructions that he be sent to Britain for treatment, but it was too late. He died at 1.35 the next morning. Later Niskanen told his nephew Ulf that the accident had broken Bikila and that, "he had died of grief."

Oddly, the next day the newspapers reported that Bikila had died aged 46. If this was the case then he would have been born in 1927 not 1932, which is the widely accepted date. Even stranger is the fact that his tomb records that he was born in 1933. However, since when he won the marathon in Rome he was reported to have been 28, which fits with him having been born in 1932, it is probably safe to assume that he was born then and thus died aged only 41.

Bikila was buried six days later, a national hero in the presence of the Emperor and with full military honours. After a service in St Joseph's Church he was buried in St Joseph's cemetery on the Debre Zeit road. Imperial Guardsmen carried his gold medals in the cortege. Yidnekatchew Tessema read his eulogy after which his grave was piled high with wreaths. Yidnekatchew said: "It is not only Ethiopia which is in mourning but the whole of Africa." A book of condolence was opened for all to sign. The *Ethiopian Herald* wrote:

Although Abebe Bikila is no more with us, his glorious exploits are written in glittering letters in the annals of sport. And he will live forever in the minds of millions of sports fans who adore him. For, had he not contributed his mighty share to the sports of his country, to Africa and to the world at large? Had he not set an example through his indomitable will and courage as to how to face hazards in life with a smiling face? Had he not, above all, been a sportsman to the core, modest in success, resolute in difficulties and unruffled in defeat?

On the same page the *Ethiopian Herald* carried congratulatory adverts from companies which extended their best wishes to His Imperial Majesty Haile Selassie 1, on the occasion of the 43rd anniversary of his coronation. But power was already slipping away from him. Since the summer it had been revealed that an appalling famine was devastating the north of the country and that officials were attempting to cover it up, to hide the disaster from the world. Over the next year a military committee called the *Dergue* began moving in on the Emperor's circle, arresting them one by one. Old and confused, the Emperor did not resist. Curiously his fate, just like Bikila's, was sealed in a Volkswagen Beetle. At dawn, on 12 September 1974, a proclamation was read deposing Haile Selassie. A few hours later, he was driven off in a Volkswagen. "You can't be serious!" the Emperor is alleged to have said when he saw the car. "I'm supposed to go like this?" He was and he did. He died, or was murdered, on 27 August 1975. The man who emerged as leader of the *Dergue* was one Mengistu Haile Mariam.

After his death, Bikila's family was helped by a philanthropic Ethiopian businessman called Abiesolon Yehdego. He had built a prominent tomb for Bikila, featuring a bronze statue of the hero. He also helped set up Bikila's widow with a sports shop in the national stadium in Addis Ababa. More than 20 years later the shop still existed, but was in an advanced state of dilapidation. Much of the floor space of the original shop had been converted into a dingy café. When Mamo Wolde died in 2002, Yehdego built a similar tomb with a statue to honour him next to Bikila.

Bikila's name is still well known in Ethiopia. Time has not dimmed his memory.

Niskanen remained in Ethiopia for the rest of his life, returning only to die in Sweden. When the revolution began, surprising as it may seem, he was actually rather optimistic. As the Red Terror took hold however, Niskanen's illusions about it were shattered. Many of his old Ethiopian friends were arrested and executed. Niskanen, who had once shone so brightly on the Addis Ababa social scene, faded, not quite into obscurity, but well into the background. He felt that the chaos that was engulfing Ethiopia was setting his life's work to naught. He also worried about his property in Awasa, and whether it would be expropriated by the new communist regime. In Addis Ababa, Niskanen lived by this stage in a large house with a large compound.

Haken Landelius, then secretary-general of *Radda Barnen* – Swedish Save the Children, has these recollections of Niskanen's last few years. He remembers his deteriorating health. "His heart and lungs were weak ... He did not have many unbroken bones in his body after all his intensive years. He was like a locomotive. Impossible to stop." He adds:

> He had planned to settle down in Awasa. The new house was completed and his house in Addis was confiscated. That did for him. He was burned out. He moved to the Building College. Soon the garden flourished and his home was the same meeting point as it had always been. He took his sauna with him, of course.

Despite these setbacks, Niskanen was not forgotten by the new generation. In fact, he had been in Ethiopia for so long that he had probably known half of them since boyhood. Mengistu himself, and several other members of the *Dergue*, had passed through Niskanen's hands at one time or another. So, it comes as no surprise to learn that it was Mengistu's half brother, Kassa Kebede, who was a minister, who now invited Niskanen to take care of a new scheme to help homeless children. It was one of his last projects.

It was in about 1980 that his health really took a sharp turn for the worse. Niskanen, who had always smoked, was chain smoking now and developed the classic smokers' disease of emphysema, which leaves the sufferer short of breath. His condition was aggravated by the high altitude of Addis Ababa. He did not want to return to live in Sweden and wanted to die in Ethiopia. However, his illness meant that, in late 1983, he was forced to return home. He stayed for part of the time at his brother Erik's house in Uppsala but also spent time in hospital, on oxygen. At a certain point, in a wheelchair, he attended a party thrown by Barbro Ergetie, the Swedish wife of the former trainer, Belete. She had worked as both a journalist and publicist. She recalls:

> He took my hand and asked me for the third time to write his memoirs. He had asked me in the sixties, the seventies and now once more. I didn't want to do it. He regretted very much that he hadn't written his memoirs. He wanted to be famous. He wanted to be on the front page.

Despite being so sick, Niskanen insisted on returning to Addis Ababa. He had an important engagement. He had to help organise and attend a marathon in the Ethiopian capital in January 1984 in honour of Bikila himself. Once there he fell ill, contracted pneumonia and was taken to hospital. He spent a week there. He was then flown, in an air ambulance, back to Sweden. Before falling into a final coma, he was visited by Haken Landelius: "I was on my way to Addis. I promised Onni that I would visit him immediately I got back. He smiled faintly. I realised that he knew that that occasion would never arise." Niskanen died on March 20th. On April 9th Marianne Sautermeister, his niece and one of Sweden's first ordained women priests, conducted his funeral in the church of Solna, the northern suburb of Stockholm to which his father had taken him in 1913.

A Note on Sources

Svenksbladet, the Swedish community in Ethiopia's newspaper and publications of *Duvbo* sports club in Sweden were invaluable because Onni Niskanen regularly updated both on what he was doing and with news about Bikila. The English-language newspaper, the *Ethiopian Herald*, is also a rich source of detail. In addition, I also used British and French newspapers and the *New York Times*. A complement to the printed sources were the interviews, which were all done in 1997 and 1998. The following is a list of most, but not all, of the interviewees. I would like to acknowledge my thanks to all of them. The spellings of some Ethiopian names may vary in different places because of different ways of transliterating them. At every Olympic games an official film is made. These are fascinating and many of the clips of Bikila can now easily be seen on the web.

ETHIOPIA
• *Abebe Wakjira*
Competed in Rome alongside Bikila and came 7th in the Marathon. In old age he lived in relative poverty in the town of Fiche.
• *Dr Woldemeskal Kostre*

Ethiopia's national athletics coach, who remembers Bikila and Niskanen well.

- *Wami Biratu*
Contemporary of Bikila. Marathon runner, member of the Imperial Bodyguard and friend.
- *Col Bekele Gezaw*
Head of the Imperial Bodyguard Sports Department in the 1960s. Knew both Bikila and Niskanen well.
- *Hailu Abebe*
Athlete, contemporary and friend of Bikila.
- *Yohannes Tadesse*
Close friend of Ragnhild Wahlborg, the Swedish nurse who loved Niskanen.
- *Lars Leander*
In 1997, a Senior Programme Officer at the Development Cooperation Office of the Swedish Embassy in Addis Ababa. He remembered Niskanen well from a previous tour of duty.
- *Tesfaye Shiferaw*
In 1997, Secretariat Head, Ethiopian Olympic Committee.
- *Tadele Yidnekatchew Tessema*
His father was the leading light of Ethiopian sports in the 1960s and 1970s and was the leader of the Ethiopian Olympic delegations to Rome, Tokyo and Mexico. Tadele has written a book about his father, which is published in English and which contains important information about Rome. Tadele is a rich source of information about both Bikila and Niskanen.
- *Professor Sven Britton*
In 1997, he worked at Addis Ababa's Leprosy Hospital of which Niskanen was director. He remembered him

well and used to go to his parties.

• *Grigory Missailidis*
Garage owner and former rally driver. He competed in the Ethiopian Highland Rally races of the 1960s with Niskanen.

• *Roman Reta*
Niskanen's cook for 33 years. Privy to all his secrets.

• *Berhanu Negussie*
Niskanen's guard and gardener.

• *Ejigu Damtew*
Niskanen's second guard and gardener.

• *Arne Carlsgard*
Swedish development expert. He was head of Swedish development volunteers in the early 1970s and had contacts with Niskanen.

• *Per Tamm*
In 1997, the current representative of *Radda Barnen* – Swedish Save the Children. He remembered Niskanen from the 1970s and 1980s.

• *Teshome Legesse*
In 1997, the administrator of *Radda Barnen* – Swedish Save the Children in Ethiopia and custodian of Niskanen's remaining photo album.

• *Tariku Abekira*
Minor member of the Imperial family. Remembered Niskanen's appearances as Father Christmas at the Emperor's Christmas parties during the 1960s.

• *Moges Shewakena*
Orphan who received financial help from Niskanen over several years which enabled him to study.

• *Abiesolon Yehdego*
A wealthy businessman and sports patron. Knew Bikila

and, after his death, gave financial support to the family. Sponsored a book in Amharic about Bikila and paid for his tomb and that of Mamo Wolde.
• *Tafari Wossen*
Film director and journalist. Worked in the government press department in the early 1970s.
• *Dr Richard Pankhurst*
Renowned scholar, former head of Addis Ababa's Institute of Ethiopian Studies. Has lived in Ethiopia, on and off, since the 1950s.

Mamo Wolde: Several requests were made to the Ethiopian authorities to see Mamo Wolde, but they were unsuccessful. In 1992, he was jailed for his alleged participation in a killing during the Red Terror, Ethiopia's Stalinist witch-hunt. He knew as much as anyone alive about Abebe Bikila. He admitted being present at the killing, but said that he had been forced to go and that he had not taken part in it. In 2002, he was convicted for six years for the crime but released on the grounds that he had already spent nine years in jail. He died a few months later. A fascinating article on the trials and tribulations of Mamo was later written by fellow runner Kenny Moore called *The Ordeal of Mamo Wolde*, which is easy to find on the web.

SWITZERLAND
• *Fekrou Kidane*
A former sports journalist and secretary-general of the Ethiopian Olympic Committee, he knew both Bikila and Niskanen. In 1997, he was Director of the Executive Office of the President of the International Olympic

Committee in Lausanne and its Director of International Cooperation and Public Information.

• *Alain Lunzenfichter*
In 1997, a senior journalist at *L'Equipe*, marathon runner and author of *Le Roman de Marathon*, published by the International Olympic Committee.

ITALY
• *Donato Martucci*
By 1997, he was retired. He was press chief of the Italian Olympic Committee during the 1960 Olympic games. He also co-wrote the script of the official film of the Olympic games.

• *Dr Primo Nebiolo*
In 1997, he was President of the International Amateur Athletics Federation (IAAF), a member of the International Olympic Committee, President of the Fédération Internationale du Sport Universitaire (FISU), President of the Association of Olympic Federations and President of the Italian branch of the IAAF. He saw Bikila win in Rome and Tokyo. A controversial figure, he died in 1999.

• *Giacomo Mazzocchi*
In 1997, he was Director of Communications of the IAAF. As a then young sports enthusiast he has vivid memories of the Rome Olympics.

• *Luciano Barra*
In 1997, Sports Director of the Italian Olympic Committee.

• *Flavio Salvarezza*
In 1997, he was the organiser of the sports club *Marcia Club Centro Lazio*. An important figure in the small

world of Italian sports politics. He has helped organise Rome marathons including one named after Bikila.

• *Franco Fava*
Former Olympic marathon runner and later a journalist with *Corriere Dello Sport*.

• *Ottavio Castellini*
Castellini is a historian of the marathon and a sports statistician. He was to work closely with the IAAF.

SWEDEN

• *Erik, May-Elisabet & Ulf Niskanen*
Erik is Niskanen's only surviving brother, May-Elisabet his wife and Ulf their son, Niskanen's nephew. They all have vivid memories of Niskanen, Bikila in Sweden and their visits to Ethiopia.

• *Belete & Barbro Ergetie*
Belete began his career as an Ethiopian trainer and sportsman. An educated military man he is now retired in Stockholm, where he lives with his Swedish wife Barbro. Both knew Niskanen and Bikila.

• *Margareta Enghardt*
A physiotherapist who treated Bikila, at Niskanen's request, after his return to Ethiopia from Stoke Mandeville.

• *Curt Erik Dahlborn*
A former policemen and friend of Niskanen's. He lived in Ethiopia from 1946-77.

• *Carmen Rubin*
Close friend of Niskanen, his ex-wife Mary and Ragnhild Wahlborg.

• *Magnus Ehrenstrom*
A military officer in Ethiopia from 1958–61. His

friendship with Niskanen continued after he became head of *Radda Barnen* – Swedish Save the Children.

• *Professor Sven Rubenson*

Arrived in Ethiopia at the same time as Niskanen and stayed for the rest of his working life. Sweden's foremost academic on Ethiopian affairs.

• *Roland Axelsson*

Lived in Ethiopia between 1964 and 1970 but continued to have a close association afterwards. As an administration officer for the Swedish government aid organisation, SIDA, he rented Bikila's house from him.

• *Tore Meijer*

Long-time resident in Addis Ababa and friend of Niskanen. In 1998, he used to help out at the Ethiopian Embassy.

• *Benhard Lindahl*

Lived in Addis Ababa twice during Niskanen's time and kept copies of *Svenksbladet*, the newspaper of the Swedish community at the time in Ethiopia. He provided copies which he translated and which are used as sources here.

BRITAIN

• *Basil Heatley*

Basil Heatley came second to Bikila in Tokyo in 1964, sprinting to a silver in a spectacular finish after overtaking the Japanese, Kokichi Tsuburaya.

• *Brian Kilby*

He ran against Bikila in Rome, Boston and in Tokyo where he came fourth.

FRANCE

• *Alain Mimoun*

Marathon star of the 1950s. Still lives in France.

• *Rhadi Ben Abdesselem*

Came second to Bikila in Rome. He died in 2000. He was interviewed by phone in Morocco.

• *Robert Parienté*

Former journalist at *L'Equipe*. He has written books about the marathon and was in the helicopter which followed the course of the Rome marathon in 1960.

JAPAN

• *Kihachiro Onitsuka*

The Chairman and director of Asics sportswear. He made Bikila his first pair of running shoes. He died in 2007, aged 89. Interview by Renaud Girard.

SELECT BIBLIOGRAPHY

Abebe, Tsige. *Triumph & Tragedy* (Addis Ababa, 1996)

Allen, Neil. *Olympic Diary: Rome 1960* (London, 1960)
Olympic Diary: Tokyo 1964 (London, 1965)

Hache, Françoise. *Jeux Olympiques: La Flamme de l'exploit* (Paris, 1992)

Kapuscinski, Ryszard. *The Emperor* (London, 1983)

Lechenperg, Harald. *Olympic Games, 1960: Squaw Valley–Rome* (London, 1960)

Lentakis, Michael B. *Ethiopia: A View from Within.* (London, 2005)

Lockot, Hans Wilhelm. *The Mission: The Life, Reign and Character of Haile 1* (London, 1992)

Lunzenfichter, Alain. *Le Roman de Marathon,* (Lausanne, 1996)

Wahlborg, Ragnhild. *Our Way to a Better Life* (Unpublished mss. ND, approx. 1975. A translation of Mina tio an i en lepraby / My Ten Years in the Leprosy Village which was published in Sweden.)

Yidnekatchew, Tadele. *Yidnekatchew Tessema (1921-1987): In the World and in the World of Sports* (Addis Ababa, 1997)

Zewde, Bahru. *A History of Modern Ethiopia: 1855-1974.* (London & Addis Ababa, 1995)

DONATION

Part of the proceeds from the sales of *Bikila: Ethiopia's Barefoot Olympian* will go to *Radda Barnen*, Save the Children Sweden in Ethiopia. Onni Niskanen, Abebe Bikila's trainer, was at one point in his long and varied career the director of the charity in Addis Abba. He advised the charity until his death in 1984. The charity describes the background to the mission thus:

> Children in Ethiopia are growing up in one of the world's poorest countries. Most Ethiopians still earn a living from the land, and even in a good year millions of families cannot produce enough food. In years of bad harvests, hunger quickly escalates into food crises with widespread malnutrition. This is made worse by lack of access to services such as healthcare, education, water and sanitation. In addition, the HIV/AIDS pandemic is sweeping Ethiopia; it has the world's third highest number of people infected with HIV. Harmful traditional practices like early marriage and female genital mutilation are widespread.

Save the Children Sweden is part of the International Save the Children Alliance, the world's leading child rights organisation, and has been present in Africa since the 1960s. Its regional offices in Kenya, Senegal and South Africa provide support to more than 100 hundred partner organisations in 27 African nations.

Save the Children Sweden fights for children's rights and delivers immediate and lasting improvements to their lives worldwide. Save the Children Sweden is guided by the fundamental values expressed in the UN Declaration of Human Rights and the UN Convention on the Rights of the Child. It works to build a child-friendly society and focuses mainly on bringing about lasting improvements for children in difficult circumstances.

Save the Children Sweden is a registered charity.
Please send donations to:
Save the Children Sweden, SE-107 88 Stockholm.
Tel: 0046 8-698 90 00
For more information visit the website:
www.rb.se/eng

REPORTAGE PRESS is a new publishing house specialising in books on foreign affairs or set in foreign countries: non-fiction, fiction, essays, travel books, or just books written from a stranger's point of view. Good books like this are now hard to come by – largely because British publishers have become frightened of publishing books that will not guarantee massive sales.

At REPORTAGE PRESS we are not frightened of taking risks in order to bring our readers the books they want to read. Visit our website: www.reportagepress. com. Five per cent of the proceeds from all our books go to charity. You can buy further copies of *Bikila: Ethiopia's Barefoot Olympian* directly from the website, where you can also find out more about our authors and upcoming titles.

Order copies on line at www.reportagepress.com
or visit any good bookshop.

REPORTAGE PRESS